Isabelle's Attic

The Story Of A Young Jewish Girl's
Survival Against The Nazis

by

Isabelle Teresa Huber

~ With Nan Miller ~

Mazo Publishers

Isabelle's Attic

ISBN 978-1-936778-27-0

Published by
Mazo Publishers
POB 10474
Jacksonville, Florida 32247 USA
USA: 1-815-301-3559

Website
www.mazopublishers.com

Email
mazopublishers@gmail.com

Cover and Page Layout
Frumi Chasidim

*In loving memory of
my mother, Frieda*

⁓⌁⁓

*To
Michelle, Chris, and Ringo (Glenn)
and
Kylie, Tatum, Sidney, Emma, and Katie*

Contents

About The Author

Most of Isabelle Teresa Huber's Holocaust involvement through the years consisted of being mute about it. After attending the "1st Children of the Holocaust" meeting in Los Angeles in the early 1990s, as a much older person, she finally began to associate herself as a Holocaust survivor. Up to that point she did not feel she "belonged" to that group of people.

Finally able to confront her truths, the flood gates opened. Isabelle, with the help of her mother's visits and carefully recorded audio-tapes, began to uncover her own hidden, repressed nightmares. Her stories began to surface, one after another, but she did not have the confidence to take them from the verbal telling to the written page.

Now, at age seventy-four, she can't stop talking about it seriously. Previously, it had only been cocktail party shock treatment. She relishes being assessed as "looking too young to be a Holocaust survivor."

Encouraged by her family to take the risk, she accepted an offer from her close friend, Nan Miller, to dictate her life-story. Through this collaboration she has now given her children and grandchildren meaning to the idea of how dear life really is.

Although born Jewish, Catholics played the biggest

role in Isabelle's life. She grew up in Brooklyn, and then moved to Los Angeles. She also lived in Anchorage, Staten Island, San Francisco, and Honolulu, before returning to Los Angeles in 1973 during her husband's medical education and residencies.

Family vacations with three teen-age children included trips to Haiti during Papa Doc's ouster, Chi Chi Castenango, Guatemala, when their hotel was blown up, and to Jordan, Egypt and Israel where they were almost killed more than once.

Today, Isabelle lives in the college town of Claremont, California with her Catholic husband, of forty-eight years, two alpacas, fifteen chickens, eight parrots, two peacocks, and geese and ducks on two acres of land. She has three grown children, in their forties, and five granddaughters and very few relatives.

An accomplished concert pianist, Isabelle speaks several languages, and considers her best asset to be a "people person."

While her motto is, "my cup is always half-full," Isabelle's life has always teetered on the edge of possible disaster. This memoir dares you to come along and feel her courage.

Acknowledgments

First of all, I would like to thank, from the bottom of my heart, my dearest friend, Nan Miller, without whose help, this book would not have been written. It was her insistent and consistent kick, (a trait I do not possess), which allowed and paved the way for me to let it all out.

Next, I want to sincerely give credit to my husband, Don Huber, M.D., who spent long hours with my mother taping her stories, and thereby, my story. I truly thank him for providing me with a life that restituted my traumatic beginnings.

I am most grateful to my mother, Frieda Pearlmutter-Landman, Hauser, Lustig, for her accurate and detailed accounts of our fall from pre-war prominent stature to one of gut-level survival. She, alone, gave me the inner self-worth impetus to accomplish "... whatever you choose to attain in life – you can do it!"

It is dear Meva Dobrucki and her family that I am forever indebted to, for their unselfish heroism in the life-threatening position they chose by loving me, keeping me safe and returning me to my mother. Without them there would be no Isa and no book.

Reuniting with my savior, Meva in 1995 brought media attention and an Emmy award-winning documentary,

"Isabelle's Attic", produced by Kyra Phillips, then a reporter for Channel Two News. Thank you, dearest Kyra Phillips, for unlocking my life-long secret terror and giving me courage to share it with the world through your documentary.

To all other Holocaust survivors, thank you for giving me the courage to share and the chance to compare my experiences with those of so many others. I feel I have been able to live my life in a much more positive attitude, as a result of it, and to realize how much easier the first part of my life was in comparison to so many.

To Chaim Mazo, my publisher, I thank you for making the process of finding a publisher so reassuring on my first try. The immediate response to my submission quieted my fears that no one would be interested in reading my memoir. Your system of consistent communications and suggestions for improvement are positive, knowledgeable and easy to follow. I couldn't have found anyone better to understand the Holocaust mentality. You have taken my realities to a recognizable level where others can grasp the meaning of emotional awakening.

I.T.H.
2013

Foreword

On March 19, 1939, little Isa Hauser was born into the wealthiest family in Czortkow, Poland. Five months later, baby Isa, also called Inka, Inochka and Inus, and her parents, Frieda and Solomon Hauser, lost their wealth and were evicted from their home, and forced into the Czortkow Ghetto by the German Gestapo.

In 1942, at the age of three, in the midst of the Holocaust atrocities, Isa's father slid her down an abandoned air-chute in the ghetto into the arms of a Polish girl, Meva Dobrucki, who snuck her home and hid her in the family attic until she could be reunited with her mother.

Isa, at age 4.

This is the story of Isa's survival against the brutal Nazis.

Prologue

The house is shaking. Lights flash and the explosions from the bombs are deafening. The drone of German airplanes churns my stomach into nauseous knots. People below are screaming and running ... houses are burning. I am invisible to the chaos surrounding me. I want my mommy! My hand reaches out to touch my reflection. The little face in my attic mirror stares back, in fear. I want to climb inside the mirror to comfort her ... to feel safe ... but she is cold. She knows the danger that grips our attic refuge. I cannot move ... I cannot make a sound ... I cannot even find a pillow to hide under. And yet this is my only safe place. A single tear escapes from my reflected self and we wipe it away as I surrender and coerce us into my fantasy, escape world.

My childhood formed, developed and survived in this isolated attic for three years. For sixty years thereafter, I refused to go back to my beginnings, excitingly dangerous beginnings in a land where Jews, for centuries, had been discriminated against and hated. I was born, hidden and one of only three Jewish children known to survive the holocaust in the town of Czortkow, Poland.

A trip sponsored by Stanford University, in 2007, took my husband, Don, and me from Vladivostok to

Moscow on the Siberian Express. In my monthly phone conversation to Meva Dobrucki, the person responsible for saving my life, I mentioned that we would be coming to Moscow. She said, "As long as you are going to be in my part of the world, we must reunite."

My stomach seized and my throat tightened as I replied, "Well, we'll see." I was still terrified at the thought of returning to Poland. My mind raced and my standard defensive phrase rose up. I got out of there once with my life, let's not push it.

◆ ◆ ◆

As the train rolls across the Siberian tundra, mile after mile of sameness numbs my apprehension of returning to Poland. Thoughts of Meva, my savior, make me realize I am no longer that scared child. I realize I don't really care anymore what Poland's attitude toward Jews might be. I am here to see Meva. I am determined to let go of my long-held fears of swastikas flying in the breeze or leather booted, black uniformed SS marauders threatening my safety. Even though I am excited about spending time with Meva, I know that a deeper pull has brought me back to Poland; I want to validate the reality of my past.

My mother, Frieda Pearlmutter-Landman, Hauser, Lustig, always talked so much about our position in the town of Czortkow; "who we were" and the properties that we had owned. Once and for all, I decided I could and I wanted to see these things.

As I am sitting in this luxurious train compartment, my thoughts drift back to my experiences in cattle cars and overcrowded freight trains as a child, fleeing in terror from Poland under the rumblings of approaching Communism. I always seem to be sickly during these "runs for freedom" train rides. This trip seems to be no exception. I am crashing downward with a nasty flu.

Our train attendant comes by to tend and tidy our compartment. He notices I am quite ill and brings me chicken broth, insisting that I need to drink it immediately. After one day of his pampered attention I am recovering and I so appreciate his genuine concern for my health.

I finally have found a good Ukrainian. He is so warm and truly worried about me. Could this man have been capable of turning me in to the Gestapo had we met during WWII? Thoughts like this still haunt me. This is how I look at people. Was his father involved in the "pogroms?" Oh, what difference does it make? He is treating me beautifully and that is all that matters at the moment.

I am amused that we can communicate in his native language. Slavik languages continue to play like well-known melodies, flowing easily off my tongue. My mother was fluent in the Polish, Russian and Ukrainian languages. It is a familiar sound to my ears. I feel strangely at home.

We arrive in Moscow and tour the city. From Moscow we fly to Lvov. The name Lvov sends chills up and down my spine. From my mother's stories, I have always pictured it as the Paris of Poland, yet now it is a dirty, ramshackle city...

My New York City-based half-brother, Joel Lustig, has also come to meet us in Lvov. He has spent the previous week searching for information about his father's, Joachim Lustig's, background. We all meet up with Meva and her son, Tomek, who drives us to the town of Czortkow.

As we approach Czortkow I am having a feeling of expectancy. I feel like I am in a flash-back movie sequence and its coming alive in vibrant, eye-blinding colors.

This sojourn becomes one of my most memorable undertakings. I discover so many things about my family that even my mother did not know.

Chapter One
Journey Into My Past

A s a beginning to our journey into my past we first take a tourist detour to see a certain famous old synagogue in Lvov. It had been the biggest and most famous Jewish hub in the city. We are hoping to find a few vestiges of the very prolific Jewish life of pre-World War II. We have a map with all of the street names and we locate the corner where the synagogue should be, but it is empty. We think we were looking for a building, and when we realize the site is barren, we need confirmation that this is the correct location. We eventually find an old man who should have known of its existence and ask him about the synagogue. He just looks at us and says. "I thought we got rid of all you Jews." *Anti-Semitism lives!*

On our own we find the remains of the synagogue. All that is left are bits and pieces of the foundation. An iron fence surrounds the foundation and has a plaque attached to it. I take a picture of this plaque and when it is later developed, strangely enough, two swastikas appear in my photograph that my naked eye had not seen when looking directly at the plaque itself.

This is very eerie ... one invisible hand painted it and time has wiped it away ... but the plaque knows.

From Lvov we travel on to Czortkow, the town where I was born. There are no hotels or motels. Meva's son, Tomek, arranges for us to stay with two Polish priests; Father Joseph and Father Michael. Even though we are in the Ukraine, the Catholic diocese maintains these two Polish priests to care for the few remaining Poles in the region. Their housekeeper warmly receives us and presents us with a beautiful lunch. We spend a good part of the afternoon listening to the priests' stories of how haunted the house has been. The haunting had consisted of footsteps, doors opening and closing, and religious papers disappearing. The house had been built by a Jew. After the priests had experienced several haunting episodes they built a small chapel on the premises to stop the haunting.

Father Joseph is so totally down to earth. How could he honestly believe that by building a chapel onto this house, all the Jewish hauntings could simply disappear? That by putting "little Jesus" on display could erase the haunting overnight? But both these priests are convinced it has.

The property also contains a small Jewish cemetery dating back to the 1700s. There are still little pieces of paper, such as you see in the "Wailing Wall" in Jerusalem, stuck in many crevices of the remaining headstones.

Jews have obviously lived in this area for a very long time.

Father Joseph agrees to join us on our expedition through Czortkow. We try to find someone who knows of my family, the Pearlmutters. Father Joseph knows of one ancient woman who knew of the family, although she herself had never had any dealings with any of them. She gives us the name of a man whose father had worked for the Pearlmutters. We then go to see this man. He looks like he is well over a hundred years old and his face is a map of his life-long ills.

I say to him through Father Joseph, who speaks Ukrainian, "Pleased to meet you Vanya, I am Inochka. I come from the Pearlmutter family."

With a look of awe and dropping to one knee, he takes my hand and kisses it saying, "During the time my father worked for your grandfather, I was just a little boy. To me, you are the next best thing to royalty."

That's how people in Czortkow saw us Pearlmutters; the reigning family.

We continue to talk and explore the past. "I remember the name of the housekeeper that my grandparents had. Her name was Tekla."

A strange sideways grin appears on his face as he gives me some shocking news, "Your grandfather, Wolfe Pearlmutter, and Tekla produced an illegitimate child. That union generated a half-Jewish child whose name is Pavel."

I heard myself thinking, this is just one example of Wolfe's amoral approach to life.

During our visit Vanya also phones the owner of the land just below him, on which stands the only flour mill in Czortkow. I had once been willed this mill, at birth, by my grandfather.

I am introduced to Yvanko, and when he hears that I am the granddaughter of the Pearlmutters, he also drops to one knee and kisses my hand. A dark shadow slips across his face and I immediately sense his obvious concern. He thinks I have returned to reclaim my property.

Not me. I know very well that people who have tried to reclaim their properties in the now Ukraine, disappear, never to be heard from again.

"Meva, tell him not to worry. My only interest is to *see* it, not to claim it."

At that point he relaxes and gladly opens the locked mill and invites us all in. He carefully takes a small wooden wheel[1] from part of the machinery saying, "For you, Inochka, because it *was* yours."

The wooden wheel the author was given from the mill.

The feeling I have when I see the mill is exhilarating and breathtaking.

My mother always talked about the mill because it had been such a huge moneymaker. To actually be standing here and to touch pieces of the mill is like finally experiencing all the dream pictures I have held in my head all these years ... it is suddenly reality and right before my eyes.

My brother, Joel, acts as though it was his mill. He is so excited and jumps from spot to spot exclaiming, "Wow, look at all these fabulous pieces of wood. The rafters are so huge. It has survived so well all these years. I can't believe how new it looks. Aren't you excited?"

I can't answer you. I resent having you here. This was

---

1. I brought the wooden wheel home, shellacked it, and pasted a picture of Joel and me onto its surface. It still sits on my desk, at home in California.

The author and her brother, Joel, at the mill.

never a part of your life ... this was my life. What the hell are you doing? You don't belong in this part of my life. You have nothing to do with the Holocaust. You are a Lustig. Lustigs have nothing to do with Pearlmutters or Hausers. We are both from the same mother, though ...

Later, as we are standing at one of the massacre locations of the infamous camp of Auschwitz and the site of the motto *"Arbeit Macht Frei – work makes freedom"*, a huge chill races through me and I suddenly feel the urge to cry out ...

"Oh, my God, I have to save my little brother."

I look around and he is standing a few feet away from me. I grab his hand and pull him closer to me as if I were trying to protect him.

"Yes, Joel, I *am* excited to share all of this with you."

After we leave the mill we continue on to the house of my grandfather's illegitimate family. Pavel's son, Boris, lives here and is now the mayor of Czortkow.

Since we are coming to meet the mayor of this town, I assume he will be well-dressed, business-like and formal. His house is well above the area's standard and yet in my reality a bit unassuming and small. As we approach the front gate, a burly peasant man, wearing a khaki cap, which partially covers his eyes, bursts out of the front door. His red-quilted hunting shirt is stretched tightly across his bulbous belly, forming a series of fleshy protrusions.

He comes out with a scowl on his face as if to say, "Who the hell are you people?" Father Joseph and Meva, speak to him in Ukrainian. I have difficulty understanding what is exchanged in this conversation, as to who we are, but the scowl is soon replaced with a smile and the next thing I know, he puts his arm around me and we all walk into the house. Within minutes, his wife appears, having just come home from work, and she also mimics the same initial look whispering to her husband, "Who are all these strange people?"

Once she is given an explanation, she also breaks into a warm smile, puts her arm around me and kisses me. She excuses herself, runs into the kitchen and prepares a feast for us all. There are platters of kielbasa, cheeses, crackers, and vodka. The mayor, Boris, disappears into another room and returns carrying a stack of picture albums. There is a picture of Tekla.

My grandfather must have been blind. She is so ugly with a scary, tight-lipped, angry face.

There is another picture. It is of Tekla's son, Pavel, Wolfe's illegitimate son. I hadn't known he even existed until the old man living above the Mill had just told me. I am looking at a picture of a half-brother my mother did not know she had. In this picture Pavel looks entirely different from the rest of this family. All of the other pictures depict features of high cheek bones, bulbous noses, short stature, and are extremely peasant-like, Slavic looking. Yet, Pavel stands two-heads taller than everyone else, has wavy jet-black hair and is very handsome with delicate features.

We remain there for most of the afternoon.

I wonder if they will tell Boris about who I am in relation to him.

At one point he throws his arm around me, lifts his vodka glass, and calls me *siostra* – sister, in a gesture of friendship.

They ought not tell him who I really am because Boris has no idea that his father was actually half-Jewish and that makes him an illegitimate grandson of a Jew.

In spite of all of this drama, we have a wonderful afternoon with this family and exchange addresses.[2]

I was anxious and would have liked to tell my mother about a half-brother she knew nothing about, but unfortunately she passed away several years prior to this trip.

The next day we travel to the ghetto of Czortkow. When I was born, in March of 1939, the city was almost on the Ukrainian border, to the East. By 2007, the borders have greatly changed. Czortkow is no longer in Poland but in the Ukraine. Many other cities that I had known to be in Poland have also become part of the Ukraine; including Lvov, the little Paris of Poland.

◆ ◆ ◆

The history of this town confirms that Czortkow, as early as 1616, had already been an established settlement for the Jews. By 1648, there was an organized Jewish

2. To date, we have not had any further contact.

Czortkow, pre-WWI.

community in existence. According to the ancient Registry of the Jewish community in Czortkow, even back then, the situation of the Jews was very hard both politically and economically. The Jews were deprived of civil rights, but were the first to carry the burden of general taxes and specific taxes imposed on Jews only. However, in the second half of the 19th century a marked improvement occurred for the Jews, both politically and economically. In 1848, the special taxes imposed on Jews were abolished and gradually they received equality of rights similar to those of the other inhabitants in Czortkow. Jews could get jobs in government offices and in law courts. In the 1870s Jews engaged in export-import trade and some even became land owners. High Schools were open to Jews and they made use of this privilege to enter liberal professions such as physicians and lawyers. These improvements pertained only to a small part of the Jewish population ... (It was during this period that my grandparents on both sides acquired their vast wealth.) However, the majority of the Jews lived in poverty and distress, struggling to earn a scanty livelihood. Eventually the Poles and the Ukrainians, although they hated one another, joined together against the Jews in order to evict them from their economic positions.

In 1914, the time of WWI, the Russians invaded Czortkow, but they did not destroy the town. The Jewish inhabitants adapted themselves to the new rulers and continued their lives as before. This Russian occupation lasted three years, and during this time an epidemic of Cholera wiped out hundreds of inhabitants.

When WWI ended, the Poles were in control of Czortkow, which lasted for about twenty years. The Poles compelled the Jews to emigrate in accordance with the well known slogan, "Poland for the Poles." They wanted to achieve this by reinstating the old taxes and not employing Jews in any government positions or general industry positions.

In the 1920s some countries were still open to Jewish immigration. Many Jews in Poland seized this opportunity to leave. Some of the most famous Rabbis of the world came out of Czortkow. It was at the time when a huge number of Jews arrived in New York – including Moishe Yankel who became my mother's and my sponsor to enter the United States. However, the gates of immigration were gradually shut, and in Poland the sources of earning a living were closed. The economic impoverishment of the Jews increased and reached its climax in the 1930s, on the threshold of WWII, which additionally brought about the Nazi Holocaust. This put an end to the physical existence of the Jewish population in Czortkow.

Chapter Two

The Crook In The Road

It was here, in Czortkow, that Meva took us all to the ghetto. She showed us the gate attachments that were still in the ground. These gates had been used to close off the ghetto area from the rest of the city. The whole area looked like a huge courtyard. Beyond the gates there was a stone staircase which led to the courtyard of the main building. We went up the steps and at the top Meva suddenly stopped, turned pale, closed her eyes for a moment and exclaimed,

"Oh my God, the last time I was here this place was wall to wall people. It looked like *Gehena*, which is equivalent to Hell. People were just lying all over the ground dying and basically waiting to be taken to their death. I had to step over bodies to reach my pre-arranged destination; the air-chute. The stench was intolerable with feces, urine and rotting bodies permeating the air. It was awful. There were absolutely no sanitation efforts to provide for the people having to live amongst such abominations! I guess the Czortkow Ghetto was no different than any other ghetto. After all, ninety-nine percent of the people from all the ghettos were eventually killed." Meva's face is blotched in tears.

This was all new to me because I had no memories of my stay in *this* ghetto or my escape. My only memory

Inside The Czortkow Ghetto.

had been a vision of a single woman standing on the
bridge we had just crossed.

*A woman is standing on the bridge, holding on to the
railing. She is sobbing hysterically and I can see her urinating.
It hits the bridge surface and splatters all over her feet.*

I have no idea why I have retained such a memory.
All I remember is my mother once telling me,
"Inochka, this is the real ghetto, the place where I
contracted Diphtheria and nearly died, as many people
did. It was a horrible epidemic that wiped out a majority
of the town. A Jewish doctor from the ghetto came to me,
like an angel, with his one remaining injection of horse
serum. This serum was the only available medication to
cure the Diphtheria. And I was the one to receive that
injection. See why I believe we were meant to live?"
My thoughts come back to the present. I shout out
to Meva and the others, "Hey, I think I remember this
bridge." Everyone is quite surprised and yet their

attentions are more directed to remaining in the moment of being in this ghetto.

I have a book from the turn of the century, showing pictures of this exact area. And in all these years, absolutely nothing has changed.

We continue to stroll throughout the courtyard until we reach "the spot" – the top of the actual air-chute that my father had slid me down and where, at the lower level in the street, Meva had caught me. I was only three years old. From there we had run to her house in the middle of the night. My mother had often told me,

"Oh Inka, you were in such bad shape. The weeks previous, when we had been hiding in a bunker, I had made you a hand-knit two-piece outfit, to keep you warm. There had been no way to change you and by the time Meva took you home, you were covered with yellow sores full of pus, and lumps. You were also full of head-nits."

We stand there at the air-chute. My brother Joel is speechless, Don has tears in his eyes, Meva trembles, her son is visibly shaken and I feel numb. My thoughts burst.

No one from the outside was allowed to enter the ghetto back then. How the hell could her parents have allowed a fourteen-year-old girl to venture into the night, enter the ghetto, walk right into the mouth of the enemy and snatch a little Jewish girl?

Meva's words spill out in stutters, "I actually put on a yellow Star of David arm band in case I was caught anywhere near the ghetto. All Jews had to wear these bands at all times. The air-chute was one floor above the ground and just inside the gates of the ghetto. It was an old air passageway and not used for anything."

Meva pauses and catches our disbelieving expressions and then continues. "Luckily, your father had a job which provided him with a pass to leave the ghetto. During one of those visits, on the outside, your father had pre-arranged with my parents to have me sneak into the ghetto. On a designated night and time, I was to take you away and hide you in our home. Your father and my parents had agreed that I, being a child, would have a better chance of not being noticed or approached. After the arrangements had been set, I remember my mother saying, 'Even if everyone else dies, we at least want to save Inochka.' I loved you, Inka, and I was willing to do anything to keep you alive."

Meva's eyes tear as she reaches out to embrace me. Stepping back she smiles and begins to recount the dangerous feat of successfully rescuing me from imminent death. At this moment my mother's words ring true again, "We were meant to live." I feel blessed as Meva describes her bravery, on my behalf.

"Inka, the deadline was looming over me and my trepidations about successfully completing the task gave me physical symptoms. My stomach tightly cramped, my toes and fingers tingled from hyperventilation and my heart beat so fast and loud that I was afraid I would faint. But saving you was far more important to me."

This confession touches me deeply and I never suspected that Meva was capable of such inner turmoil. I have always perceived her as my strong, capable protector. As she continues on with her story, my appreciation for her devotion to me deepens. Meva utters, "My mother and father reassuringly told me I would be successful in this endeavor, Inka, and kissing and hugging me, they waved me out the door and stood there as I disappeared into the night. As I walked the half-mile toward the ghetto, I prayed that the arrangements we had carefully prepared would play themselves out without any disasters. As I began to see the glow of the ghetto lights, I squeezed my pocket to be sure the arm band was there. As I approached the ghetto gates, I thought less about my fears, and the determination to save you gave me the power to stay focused."

Meva's voice is now becoming animated and we are all spell-bound by what she is recalling and physically enacting as her story unravels. "I crept over to *this* air-chute. I looked up. At first, I saw nothing and my heart dropped. I remember thinking ... Where are they? They're supposed to be on the flat, upper level of the roof area. Within seconds, I do see them approaching. A silent wave from Solomon and your mother lets me know they are ready to send you down the chute. As I position myself, I watch your mother struggling with having to let you go. She showers you with hugs and kisses. I can feel her pain. Suddenly, Solomon grabs you, turns around and gently sets you into the chute ... letting you go."

Since I have no recollection of this "great escape," I look at these scenes in my head and I can't seem to identify with this little Inka-child. Yet, Meva still holds this experience as vividly as though it had just happened. "Oh, Inka, when I saw your little feet come into view, I wanted to shout out loud. Biting my lips so no sound could escape, I grabbed you up, held you to my chest, and whispered, 'You're okay, Inka. It's me, Meva. I'm going to take you home with me where you will be safe.' Tearing off the arm band, I immediately turned and started running toward home, never looking back, never knowing how this devastating decision affected your parents."

Meva and I embrace in a long and silent knowing. Our visit to the ghetto ends in silence and we find ourselves walking out and on to the next "memory stop" without even a break, or a coffee or a chance to sit and talk about the experience.

Our next stop is my grandmother's house. It has changed greatly. Instead of being the grand three-story house of the affluent Pearlmutter's, it has become a multi-apartment complex housing several families.

As I approach and ring the bell, I turn my head to the right and to my utter amazement I find nail holes from a Mezuzah that had hung there during the pre-war days.

Why is the dent still here after all these years?

The door opens and we are confronted by a very old Polish lady. We introduce ourselves and we get the same distrustful face from her as we had received from our visit to Boris, earlier. As soon as we speak Polish to her, she lightens her expression, smiles and is quite happy to be able to speak Polish with someone. We tell her this had been my grandparents' home and ask whether she knows anything about the Pearlmutter family. She says, "I moved into this place a few years after WWII, but I had heard from other townspeople that the house had belonged to some rich Jew, before the war." We enter my grandparents' home and she is so excited we are Polish that she invites us to stay for tea and cookies.

After this visit, we continue the search for *the house*. The three-quarters of a mile walk brings us to our destination; Meva's house. As we walk along the road, I ask Meva,

"Will this road take us to your house?"

"Yes it will."

"Don't tell me when we get there. I want to see if I

can remember it."

I stare at each building we pass.

Is this it, or is that the one?

I begin to question whether I will be able to recognize it. Then we come to a strange looking area. I stop cold. There is a crook in the road for no reason. That crook somehow shakes my memory. Without looking, I point left. "If this is where I think we are, then the house should be right there."

I am pointing left without even looking at the house. "That is it! There it is! And there's my blue window."

I have found Meva's house because of the crook in the road. I recognize this spot because I sat at that blue window, day after day, waiting for my mother to come around this crook in the road and finally return to me. My mother did not come back for almost a full year after Czortkow was liberated by the Russians.

We approach *the house* and I freeze. Chills and goose bumps cover my entire body. There are two Ukrainian men sitting on a bench.

"Meva, that's the exact same bench in the garden and lilac tree that I remember Ciocia (Auntie to me and mother to Meva) sitting on. It still exists and so does the tree. But the cherry tree is gone. I remember how sick I got from picking green cherries and eating them by the mouthful. And oh, the pansies, where are they?"

Expecting a different reply she hisses at me, "I am so pissed at the Russians because they took this house away from me."

We are both tripping down in our own memory paths.

Meva approaches the two men and tells them who we are and that "this used to be my home." She also tells

Inka with Ciocia, Meva's mother.

them that during the war it was actually a safe-house where I was hidden in the attic for three years. The men say to Meva, "We too saved Jewish children."

Meva is livid at that remark. To her knowledge and from my mother's recollections, there had only been three Jewish children in that area of Czortkow who had survived. Since I was one of them, where did these Ukrainians come off saying they also hid Jewish children?

However, they seem quite congenial and invite us to come into the house, for which we are very thankful. Upon entering, we stand in the small entry way and I can look straight into the kitchen. I notice the built-in credenza that used to be on the left wall, is missing. That credenza represented many, many, hours of sorrowful pining for my mother. I would sit on a little chair right next to it. I would put my left arm straight up, holding the edge of the credenza, giving my head a place to rest sideways. This was where my mother had kissed me and promised she would come back for me. I remember that I had stood on my little chair as my mother, wrapped in a curly-haired blue coat, embraced me and gave me that good-bye kiss.

This recollection makes me feel confident and proud that I have realistic memories. My eyes keep searching to see what has remained the same and what has changed. I excitedly say, "To the left was a door that led to the attic ... the stairs to the attic were behind that door."

As one of the men opens that door for us, he apologetically says, "You will not be able to go up into 'your attic' because we sealed up the attic entry and we are using the staircase as a pantry."

Every step is loaded with food stuffs and groceries. The stairs are still behind that door leading up to the attic, except I remembered that the stairs were very deep and made of stone and cement.

I add, "As a three-year-old, it had been a major production for me to climb these stairs. Falling backwards was my greatest fear and so the ascent was made by using all fours and clutching the sharp edges of each stone step. Often, I was left with cuts on my little hands."

Now the stairs have been replaced with wooden slats. I look to the right and there is a wall rather than the French doors that had led to the salon. This salon had been the formal living room and was never heated during the winter. Now it is a separate apartment unit. "That was the room that I would quickly be taken to if a neighbor dropped by unexpectedly and there was no time to run up to the attic."

It is quite obvious how well I remember this house. I desperately want to go up to the attic. I really feel cheated because I want to compare *my* memories with the reality of that "big dark space" that had been my cozy, safe haven for three years.

Why am I reluctant to demand to go up there?

As we pass through the left doorway, leading out of the kitchen, I start naming each room as we approach it. I turn and tell Meva to ask them, "Is the cellar still here?" It is and we all go outside and lift up the cellar doors, exposing the stone steps.

This is the cellar we used as a bomb shelter. I feel the musty air brush up my legs as we begin the descent. I automatically put my arms out to grope the cold, hard, stone walls, steadying myself against the darkness.

It is so much smaller than I remember it being. I remember how I would bury my face into Ciocia's bosom and yell,

"Everybody needs to stick their head in someone's chest. It feels much safer this way."

Even as a three-year-old child I could relate to the "stick your head in the sand" concept that if you can't see, hear, and feel it ... it doesn't exist. That worked for me because after one of those bomb raids, as we came out from the cellar, the houses on each side of ours had been hit and all the occupants had been killed. I had walked back to my attic as if nothing had happened; my life simply continued. It had been spared ... I turn and ask Meva, "Do you remember Basia?"

"Oh, yes, she would literally run up this wall as far as she could, then crash down on the floor every time a bomb exploded."

Meva and I burst out laughing just thinking about that silly goat with her crazy reaction to fear. It broke the seriousness of the moment of having to relive those inevitable retreats into this cellar.

This empty space seems so far removed from my experiences, here, as a small child. Light from the open doorway casts shadows across the empty, dirt floor ... I am shaking ...

We leave the cellar and return to the house. We go toward the bedrooms and the furthest room has the "blue" window. The window from which I can still see the crook in the road – the window where I waited endlessly to catch a glimpse of my mother turning that last bend of the crook, to come back to me.

As I stand there I am not aware of anyone else's presence. It is as if I am alone, that little girl, agonizing over my need to feel my mother's arms around me. How I wish my mother could be standing here with me, now, experiencing this intense emotion.

Inka and Meva in the blue window.

How I miss my mother, still.

I sat in front of this blue bedroom window, waiting, just waiting for my mother, for eleven long months. Every day I watched people meander by with shopping bags. Cars and horse-drawn buggies would rattle by seemingly going nowhere. One day, as I stared through that window, the street remained empty. There were no cars, no movement and no people wandering along the road. Suddenly, in the distance, I saw one figure slowly trudging toward the house. As she came nearer I fixated on her blue coat; a blue coat that made me feel that something big was going to happen. When she reached the crook of the road, I don't know what possessed me, but I ran to Ciocia (Auntie) Dobrucki and said, "There's a lady coming up the road and I just know she is coming to see us." Ciocia came to the window, took one look, and passed out. It *was* my mother.

Chapter Three
The Rich Pearlmutters
And Hausers Unite

My mother, Frieda Pearlmutter, came from the richest family in Czortkow. She delighted in telling me of her childhood. Over the years during my own childhood, as well as my later years, my mother's stories often titillated and fascinated me and yet many of them evoked great sorrow. I can still hear my mother's accented voice ...

"I was the youngest of ten children and was the most outgoing, happy-go-lucky little girl. My appearance was charming with my blond hair and blue-eyes, unlike my brothers and sisters who were all dark-haired and dark-eyed. Daily life was quite easy for us. There was enough help to run the estate properly. There were maids to do the laundry, maids to keep the interior spotless and take care of all our personal needs, maids in the kitchen to prepare all the meals, stable hands to care for the animals, and there was always a hubbub of activity each Thursday evening in preparation for the Sabbath on Friday. The smell of the baking Challahs, the Sabbath bread, permeated our entire three-story mansion. On laundry days my siblings and I enjoyed the commotion of stripping the beds, rolling ourselves in and out of the linen piles, dragging the linens down the back spiral staircases and into the washing chamber as the maids called out, 'Be careful, we don't want to get into any trouble with your father.' Even though I was from such an affluent family, my father, Wolfe, insisted on checking every page of my writing tablet before he would give me the five groschen to buy a new one."

My mother would stop talking, roll her eyes in contempt and then carry on.

"Shoes were another example of my father's propensity toward being rigid and stingy. I had to show him the worn-down heels scraped to the bare sole. But I was the only sibling daring enough to tell my father, 'You are being so unfair.' His reply was, 'Frieda, you are the only one who can get away with such sassy behavior. Your sisters wouldn't dare approach me with such an attitude.' I was his pet and I knew it."

Here, my mother would pause and smugly feign a pose of triumph. Giggling and then composing herself, she resumed her train of thought.

"Now where was I, Oh yes ... I always loved to sew. One day I asked my father, 'Tato (Daddy), can I please take sewing lessons?' His reply was, 'No daughter of mine will ever stoop so low as to become a seamstress. Just keep working on your Latin instead.' In retaliation for being so dominated by my father, I went behind his back and took sewing lessons when he would travel. I would also sneak food out of the house and give it to my needy friends at school. Often during his absences I had the nerve to secretly meet up with my math tutor, Buczynski, with whom I also had an on-going romantic relationship. This involvement was a taboo as well as the fact that he was not a Jew, but a Ukrainian. This act alone was enough to be put on house arrest and get a major punishment. This man, Buczynski, went on to become a judge who was trusted by the Germans and our life-long protector. After the war was over, I was able to help him from being killed by the Russians. It was crazy escapades like this that *my* mother, your Gramma Genia, and I would keep secret from your Grandpa.

"Oh, Inochka, I absolutely adored my mother. The two of us were always in cahoots against Wolfe. It broke my heart to watch my mother, a very genteel and educated woman, being treated so unfairly by my father, the wealthy patriarch."

Genia Pearlmutter.

In later years I watched my own mother Frieda, also being treated in despicable, deceitful and dishonorable ways by her husband, my father, Solomon Hauser.

"Solomon Hauser, your father, was ten times richer than my family. One of my sisters, Rena, was married to a member of the Hauser family. Rena and her husband lived in the same nearby city as Solomon, which was Rybnik. Rena was always inviting me to her home. She knew the Hauser's had a son that was close to my age. One extremely rainy day, one of my girlfriends and I happened to be in Rybnik on a shopping trip. We found ourselves quite close to the Hauser Estate. I remember shouting, 'Rachelka, it is pouring rain. Come, we must find shelter. We are very close to the Hauser Estate. Let's run there before we get totally drenched. Solomon's parents are probably home and will be delighted to have us stop by.'

"When we arrived, the Hauser's were upset that their son Solomon was *not* home and begged us to stay, even overnight, if need be, so that I could meet him. I was sopping wet, my hair was plastered to my head, and I did not want to meet Solomon under those conditions.

"As it turned out, shortly after our arrival he came walking in from the rain, dripping wet, himself. It was love at first sight from *his* end. He was so taken by me that right then and there he said, 'You will be the next Mrs. Hauser.'

"To which I replied, 'You are too late, I already have a boyfriend.'

"Whereupon Solomon said, 'Well, we will see about that!'

"Solomon pursued our relationship relentlessly. He swore he would commit suicide if I didn't marry him. He dedicated songs on the radio and sent flowers and candy every day. Solomon begged his father to go to Wolfe Pearlmutter and do whatever it took to arrange this wedding."

My mother shook her head and dug in her pocket for her hanky, wiping her eyes and sighing.

"I already had a sizable dowry, why couldn't I marry the man that I loved? Anyway ... Mendel Hauser did meet with my father and the two men came

Young Frieda Hauser.

to a mutually satisfactory, financially based, business pact. Wolfe then informed me that I 'was going to marry Solomon.' Oh, Inochka, my heart ached because at that time I was madly in love with a struggling medical student by the name of Pino. Pino came from a poor Jewish family in town. He was not a dashing, handsome man but I loved his gentle, kind personality. I always felt very comfortable with him and my love grew from this comfort. In comparison to my scotch-on-the-rocks Solomon, Pino was milk and crackers. I had this deep, quiet, soulful tenderness for him. When my father discovered I was involved with Pino he said, 'You don't need a poor, struggling student. I can buy you a ready-made rich doctor. But now we have Solomon who is just perfect. Pino is out of the picture. You *will* marry Solomon.' My heart was broken."

Mother always stopped her story here because she invariably burst into tears and would shut down.

Back then, fathers ruled the family and daughters did what their fathers told them. All my mother's begging and crying could not soften Wolfe. My grandfather Wolfe was such a hypocrite. People thought he was

Wolfe Pearlmutter.

such a great man. Actually he was a heartless cheat. My mother's wedding to Solomon, which included renting ostentatious limousines, became one of his biggest shows. They were married in a three-day-long celebration. In addition to the hundreds of invited guests, every beggar in town was fed and entertained. Rich people used to invite the town paupers just to show their ability to be charitable. These indigents were seated at wooden tables and benches in a separate area of the garden, away from the invited guests. They were served a different but elegant meal. Their entertainment consisted of a violinist playing lively songs, allowing them to get up and dance.

The invited guests were seated at beautifully decorated formal tables with linens, silver service, and tall crystal stems. Rose petals were nestled around the bases of ornate silver candle sticks. The Russian caviar flowed freely as did the French Champagne. Endless courses of International foods appeared and were served by immaculately dressed waiters.

When my mother tells the story of her wedding to Solomon, I can visualize the grandeur of a wedding day in the life of this heiress. Her voice becomes animated and agitated.

"Frieda, wake up, it is your wedding day."

"Oh no, Clara, I don't want to get married today ... I don't want to get married at all."

"Well, we both know you have to, so let's get you up and make you beautiful. Momma will soon be here with your gown and jewelry. All our siblings and their families are here already. You should see the commotion in this house. The maids are running around with trays of fresh kielbasa and scrambled eggs, croissants ...

"Clara, stop jumping on my bed, you're crushing my legs. Okay, okay, I'll get up."

"... fresh picked berries, hot cocoa, coffee, your favorite 'rogaluch' ... let's go eat and then we can start getting you ready."

"After my sister and I nibble our fill of delicacies, Momma arrives with my voluminous, flowing gown clutched to her bosom and spilling out, hiding Momma from view. Two of her house maids have to assist her just to keep it from dragging along the floor. We trail upstairs behind them, our eyes devouring the lace trimmings, the sheen of the satin bodice, the softness of the white velvet sash, and the intricate patterns of the embroidered baby pearls surrounding the decolletage.

"Oh Clara, I know this is supposed to be the happiest day of my life but why do I have this big nothing feeling inside?"

"Frieda, he's gorgeous, super rich, so romantic and you are going to have a wonderful life. Now, let's get busy and make you look gorgeous and happy."

My mother stops the story for a moment. Tears fill her eyes and she stares into space. Recomposing herself she sighs and begins again.

"Czortkow, in 1938, had never seen a limousine. The occasional car that drove through this town was something that drew all the children out to gawk. A limo seemed like such an oddity and they had no idea what it was. I myself had never seen one, and I had to laugh as I backed myself in, as everyone guided, pushed and shoved my billowing layers of nuptial netting into this motorized carriage.

"On the way to the synagogue, dressed in my fabulous wedding gown, the limo passed a lone bicyclist. It was Pino, the love of my life. Our eyes met and there was a deep, unspoken sadness. Pino had been gone during the entire year of my engagement to Solomon. He had left to go to Switzerland to attend medical school. Jews were not allowed higher education in Poland. With Pino out of the picture for a year, the excitement of all the preparations for my fabulous wedding to Solomon had helped to suppress my heartbreak over having to reject Pino.

"But, sitting in the limo, my heart leapt back to the time I had told Pino we could no longer continue seeing each other. Through sobs and gasps I had ended what might have been a very fulfilling life. He expected as much, since he knew he was considered to be far below my stature. In that moment, in the limo, I realized how different my feelings were for these two men. I did not feel any true love for Solomon. But the love I still felt for Pino was deep in my heart. My heart kept telling me not to marry Solomon, but I did anyway. I had to. My father demanded it.

"The night before my wedding, I dreamt that my wedding veil was stuck to the ceiling, torn and grey with dirt. I knew it was a bad omen. And yet I had no choice but to go through with this marriage. I'm sure my father insisted on this union because of the great wealth that the Hauser family held."

Again my mother paused in reflection. This part of her life always brought out such regret and sadness. She then went on to recount. "Wolfe, himself, was an uneducated, hard working, self-made millionaire who had started out as the caretaker for the Landman Estate. This was my mother's property. At an early age, my mother had been widowed and left to raise four children. Eventually, Wolfe wormed his way into her bed and into her fortune. During their marriage, his acumen in business resulted in tripling the family fortune. However, his lack of social skills and ignorance as to what 'old money' could provide, prevented Genia from living a graceful life. He eventually made her existence difficult by becoming stingy, overbearing and continuously unfaithful.

"Often, during my childhood I too learned the lessons of my father's ways. When I was a little girl of eight or nine, my father took me for a ride in a horse-drawn carriage across his vast wheat fields. The housekeeper Tekla was on the ride with us. Even though I was so young, I felt something 'not kosher' between my father and Tekla. I had a beautiful singing voice and when my father asked me to please sing a song for them I refused. He threatened me."

"Unless you sing for us, Frieda, I will throw you off the carriage and you will have to find your way home alone in the dark."

"As frightened as I was of the dark wheat fields and the howling wolves, I still refused to sing for them. He stayed true to his threats and threw me off the carriage. Hysterical, and yet successful, I made it home."

◆ ◆ ◆

Here, my mother dabbed her red and weeping eyes, as she put her head back and said, "Enough for now, I'm tired."

Until the day she died, my mother remained petrified of being alone in the dark.

◆ ◆ ◆

In an old letter from my father, written in 1965, he recounted his background and *my* heritage. During that part of his life he was residing in Maracaibo, Venezuela and it was also the time of *my* first child's birth.

In the letter he wrote:

> Don't ever forget that you come from a family of highly religious and moral Rabbis and people of very high standing. My great grandfather, who my father was named after, was Mendel. That was the signet that he used in both the Yiddish and Polish languages. (At that time it was extremely rare that a Jew could possess a signet.) Mendel was a Rabbi, a writer, a physician and a grand farmer of tobacco. He also owned miles of water for his own use and supplied water to all the local inhabitants. He owned a factory for making vodka and a factory for making wooden animal enclosures. He helped discover petroleum that was located on a relative's, Wolff Backenroth's, land. That was in 1852, in the town of Schodnica. That is where I was born, Inus. (Inochka)
>
> Mr. Lukasiewicz, a pharmacologist from Lvov, helped distill the petrol and that's why the first city to be lit by means of petrol was

Lvov. Eventually, Schodnica totally burned
to the ground. In the United States, they
discovered petroleum five to six years after
my great grandfather did. My dear Inus, if
Roosevelt had not given Poland to Russia
you would have been known like a Nelson
Rockefeller's daughter. But, what worries me
at this moment, Inus, for such a happy occasion
of your first child and my first chance to be
a grandfather, I am in no position to send a
gift that is befitting my grandchild. This
is because of my temporary ruinous financial
situation caused by the local Mafia burning
down my lumber business, my surrounding lands,
and shooting me. I managed to grab my car,
drive the fifteen kilometers to the edge of
town, while bleeding profusely, and a neighbor
found me and took me to the clinic. They
only stopped the bleeding. During the first
operation I was fully awake and talking to the
surgeon. After eleven days there was a second
operation to remove the bullet. This left me
with peritonitis and so I am unable to resume
my business ventures and my normal way of life
at this time. My stomach has ended up as open
as a door. But, as you can see, God was very
forgiving to me, perhaps because in my life I
committed very few sins. God will be good to
you too, with everything you will have to go
through in childbirth, so I pray for His help
to give you an easy and happy birth.
    Forever, F

*(The letter is signed "F" because my father kept the name
Franciszek – Frank, after the real Franciszek Buczynski
procured phony identification papers for him during the war,
making Solomon's new name the same as his name.)*

How hard it is for me to believe that he could be that blind to the dark side of his character – of who he really was. The sins he committed might have been few in number but the depth of those sins was ocean deep. What made him think that he was forgiven? The only time he was involved in my life was when he slid me through the air-chute of the ghetto into fourteen year-old Meva's arms. After that he disappeared from my life and never again offered me love, interest, food and shelter, or even the slightest acknowledgment.

This letter only brought up pride in me; pride in having been born into such a distinguished family; pride in the survivorship to psychologically and emotionally put my father in his own little square and not let it interfere in my hop-scotch life in any way.

I then reread an old letter written to me by my mother, Frieda, telling of *her* life as a new bride.

She writes:

Solomon and I moved into our beautiful home, on our wedding day. I had barely one year in which to enjoy my new life. Your Gramma Genia made sure that two of my favorite maids from her estate, came with me to my new home. It was located in the best and most central part of town. It was three stories high, comparable to an American apartment house. The help lived on the top floor and the furnishings throughout the house were beautiful antique woods with handmade lace covers, crystal chandeliers and Persian rugs. It was totally done in the grand old traditional style. Genia was even willing to give me several pieces of furniture, since they had two homes. But I insisted on including some modern, sleek and sparkly decor. We had every convenience and luxury possible from

*a beautifully furnished home to all the live-in help we
needed. I decided to honestly succumb to my present
situation and to be happy with my gorgeous new
husband, my exquisite home, and all that came with
it. I was now considered one of the elite hostesses
of Czortkow. We threw countless dinner parties to
entertain the many religious and political dignitaries
who came from Solomon's side of the family.*

*You were born on March 19th, 1939 exactly nine
months after our wedding. My delivery was a
nightmare and your father started showing his true
colors. As I was hemorrhaging to near death, your
father approached me, whispering in my ear,*

*"All of this upheaval is making me very upset.
Would it be okay if I went out for awhile?"*

*As one of my best friends was on her way to our
house, she ran into Solomon with a floozy on his arm.
This was one of his capers that he would repeat and
flaunt time after time. The torn, grey wedding veil
prevailed!*

*In July, we went to my in-laws' summer home in
a town called Rybnik. It was located in the exclusive
Carpathian Mountains. We even took along one of our
maids. We stayed for two months and towards the end
of August, it seemed war was imminent and we quickly
went back to Czortkow. Then on September 1st, our
town had its first air raid. I was strolling in the street
with you, Isa, in your newly imported Rolls Royce
pram, when we heard the sirens. I grabbed you and left
the pram in the street. I ran for cover. The air raid only
lasted a short time and then with you bundled in my
arms, I hurried home, leaving the pram behind. Upon
arriving at the house we met a government messenger
with orders for Solomon to report for duty in the Polish
army, immediately. They gave him twenty-four hours*

to pack and report. I was so rattled by the sirens and
the sudden danger that the graveness of now losing
my husband to the Polish army did not really register.
Instead I just robotically helped him pack and contacted
his parents. I prayed the phone lines weren't down and
in a trembling, nervous voice I blurted out, "Oh my
God, they're taking Salo into the Polish army. I thought
Jews were not allowed to join the Polish army. What's
going on ... Does he really have to go ...? I know Salo
won't be able to handle life in the barracks."

His mother reassured me by replying, "I have
already made plans for him to be as comfortable as
possible."

Always catering to Solomon's whims and wants, and
having the money to do so, they had used their influence
to allow him to live in a hotel, instead of the barracks
and have his food brought to him so he didn't have to
eat the "mess".

He and the rest of the Polish army inductees
straggled home only fourteen days later defeated,
hungry and in tatters. But within that year, we had
to immediately start making plans to leave Poland
and go to Australia. The occupation of Czortkow by
the Russians had surprised us before we could begin
securing papers or visas. At that time I was pregnant
with you, Inochka, and we still had to obtain a passport
for an unborn child since we had decided to wait until
after the birth to leave for Australia. The name we
chose to put on the passport was Isa Hauser. You
were named after a close Uncle whose name was Isak.
When the time of birth would come, if it was a girl the
passport would be in order. If it was a boy we would
add the "k" making it Isak. This way we would not
have to reapply for a new passport.

Love always, Momma

I was glad I was born female because I don't like the name Isak. I do like my birth name Isa. Years later, when my mother would come to visit me in California, we would spend hours audio-taping her stories from our experiences of the war. One particular tape struck me straight in the heart, as at the time I had been too young to remember any of these ghastly events. In a half crying, half sobbing and wrenching voice my mother recounted her predicaments that led to her lot with destiny.

"We had lived in the beautiful house for as long as we could until we were kicked out by the Germans in September of 1939. One evening, Isa, right after I put you to sleep, the front door to our beautiful home was kicked open by four SS officers. They marched in as though they already owned our home and handed Solomon an eviction notice. It stated that we had twenty-four hours to vacate the premises. Salo, not used to being told what to do, started mouthing off to the Germans. I was aghast that he would be stupid enough to aggravate and argue with the SS. I immediately pinched his arm hard and gave him the evil eye look that meant *zatkai sie* (shut the fuck up). They cut him off immediately by saying, 'Okay, let's go to Gestapo headquarters right now if you like.'

"Oh, Isa, my destiny stepped in to save us. The fact that we weren't shot on the spot or taken to headquarters was pure luck. Salo shut his mouth, took the eviction notice and said, 'We will comply and be out of here tomorrow.'

"They clicked their heels, turned and left. I turned to Salo and shrieked, 'Those soldiers' actions were not the typical behavior of the SS. We could be dead right now. You are no longer the boss of anything. In the face of the Germans you are nobody. Do not mess with them, Salo.'

"Without another word Salo and I went about the

house gathering what valuables we could. We were one of the first families to be thrown out of our home, since we were the richest Jewish family in town."

Here, my mother totally breaks down in uncontrollable sobs. I had been so used to this reaction of hers, over the years. Now, listening to her retell her war stories, the tears and laments no longer had an effect on me. I was now able to listen to these stories without becoming emotionally entangled. I merely brought her a box of tissues and waited for her to regain her composure.

"The Germans confiscated all of our possessions and properties. We went to live with my parents as did much of the rest of the family; sisters with husbands and kids. Togetherness seemed safer. We all gathered at Genia's house in Czortkow until we were herded into the temporary ghetto sector. It was here that we began to dig a secret hideout under a built-in credenza in the kitchen. The credenza took up half of the kitchen wall. In order to come up with a secret passage way, the bottom shelf of the credenza was removable. In order to disguise this trap door shelf, we decided to use an animal statue as a decoy. Under that area we dug to make a hiding place, below ground level. Each night the men in the family would fill as many buckets of dirt as they could, take it outside and spread it out by shuffling their feet to blend it in with the existing ground. Often I could hear them disagreeing on how to get the job done. Pola's husband, Munio, said, 'I think we should dig straight down. This will prevent the Germans from hearing any hollow sounding spots on the kitchen floor.'

"The others would shout, 'No, we need to dig and expand sideways to give us enough room for everyone to breathe.'

"Inus, I had such difficulty with the precious time they were wasting. We had no good place to hide and I just wanted them to make us safe. My fear for our lives was all encompassing. I interrupted the men's meeting and reprimanded them for questioning our originally drawn plans. I yelled, 'Your squabbles have nothing to do with the danger of this situation. Your egos are getting in the way of doing what needs to be done. It doesn't matter if we glue a dog statue or the cat statue to the cover shelf. Let's just get this bunker done.'

"Seeing my petrified yet resolute face, the men looked at each other, in a stupefied way and Munio uttered, 'She is absolutely right. The Germans could come tomorrow. Let's do it as planned. No more bickering.'

"So we meticulously glued the huge reclining cat statue to the surface of that bottom shelf to make it appear normal. That bottom shelf leading to the hiding place had a handle on its underside so that it would open and shut from below. Many hiding places, throughout Poland, were being discovered because people dug straight down under floorboards and it left the boards unstable and gave off a hollow sound when tapped.

"Staying with the original plan we constructed a ladder that led from the top of the hole, down into the hiding place. Then we dug a tunnel past the outside of the house. The tunnel then turned upward to the ground level edge of an open area. There we made an opening in the ground and covered it with grass, twigs and dead plant leaves. It was my job to poke near the edge of the ground cover to allow some fresh air to enter the hiding place. All I could think about as I scraped and poked was 'God, please keep Inochka alive.'"

Again, my mother crumbled and whined, "Turn off the tape. I have to catch my breath."

And, of course here came the crying again. I had to leave the room so as not to make a negative comment about her wailing. I went and refreshed her tea cup, giving me time to control my urge to explode.

How can you cry again? You have told this story so many times. Get over it Mom. I cannot handle looking at your teary, crying, unhappy face. We no longer have a reason to be crying. Just be happy and grateful.

Composing myself I returned to the taping session, handed my mother her tea and was relieved to find her more at peace. We resumed our session and she went on to describe the rest of the hideout construction.

"A second ladder was constructed in this upward tunnel so someone could climb up and out to remove our human waste buckets. We intended this to be a place of refuge from air raids and 'actions', but made it secret in order to hide from the Germans when they came looking for candidates to be taken to the concentration camps. Most actions lasted a day. One of the actions lasted three days which surprised us and we were in no way prepared for it. We ended up with not enough water or food to last the three days. I had only brought one piece of bread and one apple.

"Oh! How cramped and unbearable it was. In our stuffy eight by six foot space, twelve bodies huddled on the cold, dank floor. The smell of dampened earth barely blocked the ghastly stench of human fright. The twenty-four-hour darkness brought on discontentment and depression. We all began to take on animalistic behaviors; pushing, vying for position and vehemently protecting our meager caches. I demanded to position myself, with you in my arms, Inochka, closest to the upward tunnel ladder so you could get what little air seeped through the tiny air hole."

"As miserable as it was, Mom, think of the positive. I don't remember it, so for me, it's like it never happened."

She defensively shot me one of her "looks" with her stern, disagreeable pout and I could tell she had no concept of what I was trying to say. Mom's perceptions were incessantly based on the fact that she felt she was supposed to suffer the rest of her life. Perhaps she felt guilty for being one of the survivors. I don't really know. So, I let go of pressing this point and said, "Okay, back to the tapes."

Mom took another deep breath and returned to her story.

"You spent most of those three days asleep and I thought you were sick or going to die from lack of oxygen, water and food. The very first night the man who was voted to empty the 'honey bucket' lost his balance half-way up the ladder and all the excrement poured out of the bucket right on top of us, Inochka. *Goteniu* (Oh my God), our bread was completely ruined and we were drenched in foul smelling feces, urine and vomit. I managed to save the apple and used the same tiny spoon that I had used on the air hole, to scrape the apple meat into pulp so you could have some nourishment. But the smell of my body and clothing was unbearable. And you, my little precious baby, were bound in dirty, rancid diapers and wet woolen tights, for three days, without any changes or cleaning. When this 'action' ended we crept back into the house and when I undressed you, your body was broken out in sores and your little tush looked like red sand paper. Life was lived from one 'action' to the next and each one produced yet another catastrophic result.

"Back when we were still residing in Rydoduby, Genia had slipped, fallen and broken her hip. The times were such that to seek medical help was a passport to German capture. My mother's hip eventually healed but she was never again able to walk without help. I can see her yet, holding on to the back of a kitchen chair and shuffling her way across the floor. Getting her into our ghetto hiding place became almost impossible.

"During one of our last 'actions', when you were about two years old, I was unwrapping and crinkling the newspaper that held a piece of stale bread, and you said to me, 'Sh, mamma, *oni mogą nas słyszyć.*' (Sh, they may hear us.) You were already well-trained in the art of being quiet."

"Weren't you lucky to have such a good kid. Otherwise, you might have had to smother me, like so many mothers had done, in order to save the rest of their family."

"I couldn't even imagine doing such a thing to you Isa. Let me go on with the story, please! I remember, one of the first 'actions' that took place before the ghetto was formed. It was in Rydoduby, during the fourteen days that the Russians had occupied Czortkow. We had shared a shelter with some of our neighbors. We would keep a couple of suitcases packed and waiting for us to grab as we ran for shelter. They contained emergency food. One time, as we scurried to our hiding place one of our suitcases was snatched by Fetchko, the son of the man who took care of Genia's and Wolfe's stables. This boy had been a trusted part of our family. My father had seen potential in this Ukrainian lad and had paid for his education to attend a formal school.

"As the air raid siren sounded, he had grabbed one of the suitcases and fled, thinking that it was filled with diamonds, gems and money. To his chagrin, it only contained food and water. He was, however, convinced that valuables were still in one of the other suitcases. So, a few days after this raid, this 'friend and neighbor' showed up at our front door with the NKVD (the penal regiment responsible for sending people to Siberia.) It turned out that the reason he never had a job was that he was a communist, and now he was turning us in for supposedly having undeclared valuables. We were sure we were ticketed for the Siberian Express. But, by now Germany and Russia were at war and the Russians had much bigger problems than us. So, we escaped being sent to Siberia. You, Inus, were only six months old and our beautiful home and my charmed life was instantly gone and now my main reason for living became gut-level survival, overnight."

Hands clasped to her chest, my mother let out a big audible sigh, "Tak... tak ..." then she turned to gaze at me saying, "So, how are your children doing, Inus?"

She tired of talking about the war ... let me see if I can still prod her on.

"So, Mom, what happened next? Let's keep this tape going, it's almost at the end of side two."

With a flattered expression at being asked to continue on, she was more than happy to comply.

"As the Russians were withdrawing to the east, the Germans were coming in from the west. It was a race through Czortkow. As the Russians withdrew they tried to destroy anything that would be of value to the Germans. The railroad station was a prime target. The station contained barrels of gasoline, and when the Russians set off their bombs, the barrels exploded. We looked up our street and saw a fireball headed our way. Everyone ran for their lives. We had to cross our street to get to safety. The fireball was almost on us when I looked back and saw Genia shuffling across the street pushing her kitchen chair. I ran to her, grabbed her and started back across the street. By now the fireball was almost upon us. I'm not sure how close it came, but I remember the intense heat as it passed by. We made it across the street. I looked around and couldn't see a familiar face. Everyone had run away including the rest of my family.

"At the same time this was happening, the Germans had surrounded the town and had come flying in on their motorcycles. It was complete chaos for Jews and Gentiles alike. Everyone was scared to death of the Germans. The Jews, knowing the Germans' hatred for them and having already heard horrible stories, disappeared off the streets as quickly as possible. This was the first 'unofficial action.' We all ran for cover. I knew I couldn't make it with both my mother and you, Isa, so I had to make a decision. It was probably the hardest one of my life ... knowing I would have to leave my mother behind. Genia also realized the quandary we were in. She told me to take you and run. I grabbed you and we ran into the hills surrounding Czortkow. We hid in the woods until early morning and then snuck back into town. I made my way through the streets to our house. We hid in our secret place for the next few days. During those few days all the members of my family snuck back into our house and into our hiding place, including my poor crippled mother.

"Meanwhile, some of our Jewish leaders formed a committee called *Judenrat*. They met with the Germans to try and set up an organization for the Jewish people. The Germans advised them to announce to all the Jews that they could come out of hiding and they would have guaranteed safety. The next morning we heard a loudspeaker announce that one woman from every Jewish household had to report for a work party at a designated spot in the little town square. The Germans would drive around the streets and bellow out instructions through a megaphone. We were assured that the women who reported would not be harmed, and would be returned home that evening.

"When they came to Genia's house, I decided I would be the person to report for work and so I offered, 'Momma, I am the logical one to go because you are too old and both of my sisters are of dark completion. I am blue-eyed and have blond hair and I speak German without an accent. Take good care of Isa, while I am away.' Since I had the most out-going and likable nature in our family, I felt my personality might offer some protection. After several protests everyone finally agreed.

"One hundred women were gathered at the town square and ten German soldiers each chose ten women and reported to a designated destination. Ironically, I was taken to my own beautiful house, with nine other women. My house was now the headquarters for the Gestapo. It was our duty to clean everything. I immersed myself in the task. There were moments, during the day, when I lost myself in thought and went about these tasks as if I were back in my own home. I was so engrossed in what I was doing that I didn't notice a young German officer who was watching me. He came up to me and touched my hair and asked, 'Are you Jewish?'

"My reply was, 'I am here with the work team, so I guess I must be.'

"He then said, 'You don't look Jewish with your blond hair and blue eyes. You're doing such an excellent job, and I was told Jewish women were dirty. Why are you doing such a meticulous job?'

"I found my tongue and my pride and I told him this was my home. At that point, the German soldier looked stunned and then said, 'You must leave and go back to wherever you came from. I can't say any more. Just get home and off the streets.'

"I was afraid to do that since I had no papers and it would be too dangerous to walk the streets. His reply was, 'You have a much better chance if you leave now. Use the alleys ... but give it a try ... and go!'

"I felt an impending terror. I left and started through the back streets. Whenever I saw a German soldier I would duck into the house nearest to me, or behind any convenient place that would give me cover. Somehow I got back to Genia and you, Isa. All the other women who worked that day never returned home. They were all shot after the day's work was over. That night approximately 350 women were killed. When Genia found out that I alone had survived that work party she said, 'I know you will survive the war, daughter.' It was then that I started planning for our survival."

Chapter Four
Eight Months Of Semi-Ghetto

The first step in survival for my mother meant ... get away from the Jews ... which included moving us into a non-designated Jewish area. From her perspective, if you're among them, then your chances for survival diminish. Her way of thinking helped us both continue living. Her recounting of the semi-ghetto period was proof that her thoughts were correct because people who stayed in the semi-ghetto were always in greater danger of being seized and killed.

Wanting to get my mother back to her storytelling I asked "Okay, Mom, how did all of this affect us?"

She resumed:

"The Germans were now getting serious about liquidating Jews. They set up a semi-ghetto and designated certain neighborhoods where Jews were restricted, but they could still move freely around Czortkow. During this period, your Gramma thought we would be safer elsewhere, rather than staying in her home. We left Gramma's house, at her insistence, and moved into a rental house across from the Dobruckis, who were non-Jewish and living in the non-Jewish part of town. We were there for eight months, but long enough for the Dobruckis to fall in love with you, Isa.

"Grandma Genia, refusing to leave her house, decided she no longer wanted to live in this fashion of having to hide and not being allowed to be a Jew. One day she stepped out of her home, sat down in her favorite chair in the garden and waited for destiny to take its course.

"Two German soldiers come into her garden and are shocked to see an old Jewish woman staring them down. Suddenly a child's cry is heard nearby, and the German soldiers ask Genia, 'Where is this baby?'

"Genia replies in fluent German, 'This child might survive and it will pay all you pigs back for what you are doing. My life isn't important to me. I am not young anymore. Here I am, shoot me. And I will not tell you where the baby is.'

"The two German soldiers look at each other and seem to feel strange about killing her. One soldier demandingly shouts, 'Get up and go back to your house.'

"Standing up, she tries to shuffle with the chair toward the house. The two soldiers continue arguing over who is going to shoot her. They're both standing with arms extended, weapons ready to fire. One says, 'You kill her.' The other replies, 'No, you kill her.' They can't seem to shoot. When she is almost at the entrance of her home, one of them does shoot ... point blank."

This horrific scene was described to my mother, Frieda, by her closest friends, Zelda and Rose, who had been hiding in a nearby bunker. They had actually seen this atrocity unravel through slats in their bunker wall. Oh, how awful.

My mother relates to me exactly what Zelda had told her ... "Frieda, the scream we heard from Genia, as she was shot, has haunted me to this day."

◆ ◆ ◆

My mother had adored Genia and had begged to stay with her. But Genia had known her daughter should get phony papers and get out of the area. Shortly after Genia's death the semi-ghetto was disbanded and the real ghetto was established. Since ninety percent of the Czortkow Jews died during the last "action" of the semi-ghetto, the survivors were told to gather at the Synagogue. My mother has often told me that when we (mother, Solomon and I) arrived there, people were kissing and crying. Others were yelling and screaming because loved ones must be dead since they hadn't arrived. This is where another of my mother's friends came running up to her weeping, "Frieda, your mother is dead."

Mother said, "Yes, I know, *Bogu Dzenki* (Thank God), she no longer has to suffer."

"Everyone was trying to figure out what to do and to either go into hiding more deeply than they were or go into the ghetto and see what would happen. Eventually my mother's sisters went into hiding. Two of them survived and one went straight to the gas chambers with her own children and her non-Jewish nanny, who insisted on going with them. We went back to our rented house across the street from the Dobruckis' house. My grandfather went to Tekla and she hid him. Then one day the Gestapo burst into our illegal house and forced us all (father, mother and me) into the ghetto."

My mother's description of this panic-stricken event leaves me with horrifying, visual scenes of how it must have gone down.

"We are sitting at the table while you, Inus, are crawling around on the floor. Salo and I have just started making a list of steps to take to acquire phony papers. We already know that the worst place we could end up would be in the ghetto. Buczynski has already warned us to do whatever it takes to avoid the transports from the ghetto. The door flings open. Looking up, I see three SS officers lunging forward, brandishing automatic weapons in our direction.

"*Rous, rous* – get out, get out!"

"Inus, come to Momma, now! Grabbing you, I stand up and say in my best German, 'Why are you kicking us out?'

"As they are wrenching Salo's arm against his back and pushing him out the door, the leader of the group approaches me, strokes your toe-head hair, Inus, looks into my blue eyes and hesitantly asks, 'Are you really Jewish?'

"No, what makes you think there are Jews here?"

"It was reported. Grab what you need, and come with us."

"Meanwhile the Dobruckis can see and hear what is happening. We don't dare say good-bye to them or even look in their direction. I know in my heart they will know where to find us. Trembling with the reality that something worse is coming, we are pushed out of the door and into a military jeep. Salo sits in silent pain. You, Inus, squirm on my lap and reach out to touch the shiny buttons on the sleeve of the officer."

"*Schine, kinder* – what a pretty little girl."

"For a split second I think we might be let out, but one of the other officers turns around and shouts in German, 'Are you stupid with your compliments? We have smashed prettier babies than her against walls. Just shut up and let's drop these damn Jews off.'

"Resigned to the inevitable, my gut is screaming ... 'you're going to get nowhere with this ... so let them drop us off in one piece and then I will find a way to get us out. We are meant to live, remember?'

"The driver slams the jeep into gear and during our bumpy and excessively rapid departure I hold on tight to you, Isa, to keep you from banging your head against the front seat as we continuously make sudden stops. Although the trip is only three to four miles in distance and the streets are empty, as everyone is petrified and in hiding, it feels surreal to me and time loses all meaning. In passing familiar houses and streets my mind cannot adjust to the gravity of this situation ... we are caught ... we are on our way to the ghetto.

"I mentally plot who to contact to help us get out of our pending doom. The very first name that comes to mind is Buczynski, the Ukrainian judge and our constant protector. He is one of ten people in this world who speaks and reads Sanskrit. With all his connections as a judge, he is able to promise me that he can and will arrange for the phony papers for us. I know that when people end up in the ghetto, they disappear and never return. This is not going to happen to us.

"The car slows and stops in front of two huge iron gates that are set into the asphalt at the edge of the street gutters. This is the entrance to what was Czortkow's marketplace. And now it will be our prison. I squeeze you closer to me, Inus, and take Salo's hand as we are pushed out of the car and herded through the gates.

"My immediate impulse is to secure the best accommodations possible. I know it will be overcrowded and very unhealthy for us. I must keep you safe, Inus, and away from the diseases. We are then told, 'Go to the registration office. They will give you your assigned quarters and brief you on the rules and regulations.'

"The officers point us in the direction we are to go and they turn to leave, leaving us standing there in the middle of what used to be the market square. It suddenly hits me. I can't believe we are this close to death. My dreams are shattered. My life is disappearing. What is going to become of us? I look down at you clinging to me for dear life and say, 'Sweet little Isa, Mommy will take care of you.'

"In my head I see the danger. This can only mean we are headed for black destiny. We are again among Jews."

Chapter Five
Tales Of The Ghetto

Years later, once we were all safely living in the United States, and I was twelve, my mother had begun to unravel and constantly talk about the war. She described to me what life in the ghetto was like.

"After our registration into the ghetto, we are shown to our quarters. Amazingly, we have the room to ourselves in a house. It is small, approximately ten by twelve feet. There is only one bed and a small table with two chairs. The three of us all live in this small room that is **ours** at first. The communal bathroom is down the stairs and at the end of a long hallway. Most of the time, the toilets get clogged and fill the air with a foul smell.

"Soon, our living quarters go from bad to worse. As more people are rounded up and crowded into the ghetto, strangers move into our little room. They are a family of six, including four young boys between the ages of six and twelve. The room becomes unbearable with noises, squabbles, and unwashed body odors. This poor family has to sleep on the floor with nothing but a blanket and yet they are grateful they have a spot where they can stretch out. The health conditions become non-existent. Food is insufficient and for some, unavailable. People all around us are dying from starvation. In order for me to secure food for us, I choose to leave the compound and take a huge risk.

"Since everybody in the ghetto has to wear the arm bands with the Star of David, I use your little dress, Inus, as a shield. I hold you in one arm, covering the arm band. I sneak out of the ghetto, illegally, and go to the 'black market' to sell what few pieces of jewelry I still have in exchange for some food. The reason I hide the arm band is because a Jew is killed on the spot if they are discovered without a band on the outside of the gates. I am half-legal because I have an arm-band but I don't want it to be showing. Outside the ghetto I can pass as a non-Jew because of my Aryan appearance. I speak Polish without any accent. A lot of Jewish people speak Yiddish at home and therefore tend to have a slight Yiddish accent when speaking Polish. Therefore, I easily pass for a Pole and am able to successfully exchange my beautiful jewelry for the food we are so hungry for.

"Salo manages to get a work permit during our registration into the ghetto. He is allowed to leave the ghetto during certain hours of the day. During his first day out he contacted the Dobruckis and set up the arrangement for Meva to take you, Inus, and hide you in their house. This is our only solution to keeping you safe and alive.

"Salo leads us through the dark passageway to the top of the air-chute. I clutch you tightly and cover your little face with kisses. 'Come on, Frieda, we must let Inochka go. We only have a few minutes more before the commandant walks his beat. Give her to me, now.'

"Oh, Salo, I am losing half of my heart, but I know that this is the only way Isa can possibly survive."

"As I release you into Salo's arms, I watch you silently disappear into the darkness of the chute. I put my hands over my mouth to muffle the rising sobs and uncontrollable wails of despair. Will I ever see my child again?"

All this talk about my mother's experiences made me build an emotional wall against all her hurt. My twelve-year-old ideas construed the war as something romantic and exciting. I thought I wanted to be a Mata Hari. I thought my life was quite boring and staid. I no longer had to hide or play games in order to stay alive. I didn't have the constant fear. I missed the Dobruckis terribly, especially Meva. I listened as my mother went on ...

"Two days after you are saved by Meva, Salo kisses me good-bye to go out of the ghetto to collect and sell iron that he scavenged. I watch him step into the street, just beyond the ghetto gates. He takes three or four paces and is suddenly accosted by two soldiers. I can hear Salo arguing with them and waving the work permit in their faces.

"One soldier shouts, 'Shit on your work permit! You're coming with us!'

"Grabbing hold of Salo's arms, both of the soldiers brandish their bayonets and force-walk him down the street toward the local jail. Leaning out of the window of our room, I gasp. I'm losing it all ... my house, my charmed life, my mother, my siblings, my baby ... and now my husband? Not only do I have to get out of this ghetto, I will need to get Salo out of jail. My list is getting longer. I am so drained. My body weakens, I become sick and I can no longer leave the room.

"While my body is burning with fever and my throat is on fire, I get word that Salo has been taken to a concentration camp. I may never see him again. I had thought that we had no cash money and find out that Salo actually wore a money belt hidden under his clothing. He told his cell-mate to get the money belt to me. He had been carrying a large sum of money around his waist all this time and had not told me. His cell-mate who brought me the money belt spent most of the cash to get out of another jam and by the time he hands the waist belt over to me, very little is left. If I had known this from the beginning we might have been able to buy our way out of the ghetto. There were some people who were actually able to buy their way out."

I am furious. How the hell could my father let my mother risk her life, without a pass, while all the time he had more than a sufficient amount of cash that, with his work-pass, would have allowed him to buy us anything we might have needed?

My mother interrupts my mind-rage by continuing the story ...

"Now it's too late and my condition worsens. I contract Diphtheria. There was a doctor by the name of Goldstein in this ghetto who was called in to see if he could do anything for me. For Diphtheria the only viable medication was to give a horse serum injection. Dr. Goldstein bent close to my ear and whispered, 'I have one horse serum injection left. You have a baby. I want you to live. Let me give this to you now. I hope it's not too late.'

"All of these ghetto doctors kept cyanide pills to take in case they were caught and tortured. Ironically, that was exactly how Dr. Goldstein, his wife and his children, died.

"I lapse into a delirious state. Thank God, I have no more pain, no more feelings, no fear ... I have floated into nothingness. Sometime during this delirium I enter a dream with my mother. I raise my arm upward toward Genia. She is hovering over me and will not take my outstretched hand. Momma, I feel a hot poker through my heart ... why will you not take my hand? 'Frieda, you will survive the war. I don't want you to join me yet. Remember, you are a survivor.' As I try to reach my mother's hand I am actually grasping onto the headboard of my bed. I suddenly jump up, feel absolutely healthy and my fever has broken. I become acutely aware of the realities of my frequent dreams. Whenever I dream of my father, Wolfe, bad things happen to me. Yet dreams of my mother, always bring goodness and positive outcomes. So, you see, Inus, I was always rescued from my worst moments by a destiny to survive this holocaust that took so many others. I was only there, in that ghetto, for two more weeks. As promised, Buczynski came through with my Irish papers. He also made arrangements to rescue Salo from the Majdanek concentration camp. Upon leaving the ghetto, Buczynski insisted that I contact him in his chambers in the town of Lvov. It was then that I came and kissed you good-bye in the Dobruckis' kitchen, Inus."

This is where my conscious-life memories begin.

Chapter Six

The Invisible Princess In The Attic

Climbing up onto the kitchen chair, I throw my arms around Momma's neck as she embraces and kisses me. Her warm tears run down my cheek.

Why is Momma crying?

I have been here with Meva for several days. I know Momma said she'd come to get me. She is so happy to see me that it makes her cry.

"Inochka, be a good girl and listen to Meva and Ciocia. Always do what they say. Most importantly, be quiet."

"I thought you were coming to take me with you, Momma."

The instant fear of being separated from Momma, once again, so soon after my rescue from what Meva calls "the chute caper" makes my lower lip quiver.

"Hush now, Inus, Momma has to leave you here, but I promise to come back for you as soon as I can."

Bending down to embrace me one more time, I bury my face in her neck. I nuzzle in the soft furry hairs of her blue curly coat and smell her familiar scent. I struggle to not let go as she pulls away. Over my head she and Ciocia speak in agitated tones. Meva has tears in her eyes and is also visibly upset.

I know Momma is coming back[1]. *Why are they so upset?*

As Meva opens the door that leads to the attic stairs she takes my hand and says, "Inka, I am going to show you your very own room. You will have your own bed. This is where you will spend most of your time. You must always be silent, as if you were not here. When you walk it must be tippy-toe and you never, ever, come down by yourself. I will come to get you when it is safe to come down."

I know how to be quiet. Mommy taught me how to hide in dark places. These steps are so high. How will I be able to climb them?

Meva seems to sense my concern in climbing these steep, jagged stairs and smiling sweetly she moves behind me and says, "Okay, Inka, crawl on all fours like a puppy and we will get you up into the attic."

I want to please my new friend. I do what she says. Meva is lifting my tush and helping to move me up the first step.

The step is cold and scratchy. It is cutting my hands and scraping my legs. I must keep quiet. How many of these steps are there? This is too hard and I can't do this by myself.

As I look up this huge mountain of stairs, it seems impossible for me to reach the top.

"Meva, carry me up."

---

1. I was supposed to have stayed with the Dobruckis for three days and it turned into three years. Their attic became my refuge and my teacher.

Grinning and picking me up in her arms, Meva and I begin the dark climb to the top.

I can see a tiny ray of light coming. I will not have to stay in the dark. There are shadows of trunks, furniture and a huge mirror. Oh, the attic is so big. There are so many new things I can play with.

I hug Meva in excitement as she sets me down. Taking my hand, once again, Meva leads me through a path of dusty, broken junk. We turn right where the light is the brightest. We are walking into a tiny room with a bed, a little table and chair and a nightstand which holds my *nocnik* (chamber pot).

There is so much light in here. It feels happy and cozy and it's mine.

I run straight to the French doors that lead out onto an iron-railed balcony. Meva jumps in front of me and grabs me before I can open the doors.

"This is your number two of never-evers, Inka. No one must ever know you are up here. You must never go out on the balcony unless Ciocia first lines the iron railings with quilts and blankets. Matka (mother) hangs our bedding out here every week. On those days you may **sit** out there, but never stand up. But not today, Inka."

Before Meva leaves me up there, she reassures me that she will return.

"I must go to school every day, Inka, but I will teach you how to read and write and I will spend as much time as I can with you, up here. At mealtimes someone will come and get you. When the meals are over, you will come right back to the attic. Never, ever, show yourself unless we come for you. I love you little Inka. We will keep you safe."

Meva turns and leaves. I can hear the attic door close.

I am alone.

I am happy and secure. I curl up on my little bed and fall asleep.

I am awake now and I am hungry. I hear dishes being rattled downstairs. I wonder if it is time to eat, but Meva has not come to get me. I want to jump up and down on my little bed, but no ... it will make noise. Carefully removing my shoes, I tip-toe out into the big, dark attic and begin to explore. The trunk in the corner is just my size. Opening it I find old dresses, hair bows, hats and lace-up shoes. They smell musty and moldy but the colors and lace are all I need to begin my imaginary dress-up fantasies. I pull out a faded pink blouse and a pink-striped angora hat. I step into the blouse and put on the hat, tying it under my chin. *I tip-toe over to where the huge, marred, mirror stands.* It has spider-like veins of black splotches all over it.

I can still see parts of myself, but why can't I see me on the black splotches? I must have missing parts?

I look down to see if the black splotches are on me. No, I am here, all of me is here.

Looking at the splotchy, pink me in the mirror, I whisper to her,

"I will call you my friend-in-the-mirror. I want to try on

another dress ... and I'll be right back."

Running tippy-toed back to the trunk I lean over and dig down into the pile of clothing. Each time I would create a new outfit to show to my friend-in-the-mirror. She was always there to admire me, listen to me, telling me how pretty I looked in my beautiful gowns and never asking anything of me. The princess was emerging.

The dishes have stopped rattling. Does this mean Meva is coming to get me? I'm really hungry now.

The downstairs door opens. Meva climbs the stairs, easily, and greets me with, "Supper is ready, let's go."

Snuggling me under her arm, she winds her way down the steep stairway and we enter the brightly lit dining room. The family is already seated. Wojcio (uncle) is at the head of the table, at one end, and Ciocia is at the other end. Janek, their son, who is Meva's older brother, is seated on the far side, up against a day bed. Meva and I sit down across from Janek. Ciocia lets Meva make me a plate while she explained our dining procedures.

"Inochka, we are so happy to share our home and our meals with you. When you are eating, you may come and be downstairs with us. If anyone comes to our door you must run and hide under the piano in Meva's bedroom. It is covered with a large embroidered shawl[2] that hangs to the floor and will keep you well hidden. Otherwise, if there is enough time, we will get you back up into your attic. Even if it is mealtime and we do not come for you, it just means it is not safe, and you must be patient and wait."

---

2. This shawl was donated to the Museum of Jewish Heritage in New York City.

The longer it takes me to eat, the longer I will get to stay downstairs with the family.

I begin to search for a specific kernel of corn. Then I go for a search of hidden treasures in a bowl of clear broth. I plop my special corn kernel into the broth and chase it around the rim of the bowl with my fork. Finding another perfect corn kernel I stab it with my fork, as Meva breaks my spell by interjecting,

"Inka, you're supposed to eat the food not play with it. At the rate you are eating, it will be time for breakfast before you finish this supper."

This is the whole idea!

♦ ♦ ♦

At the beginning of my stay with the Dobruckis, my body was infested with sores and my head festered in nits and lice. These are the gifts I brought with me from the ghetto. Endless delousing sessions, which were bloody and painful, routinely occurred each morning and each evening. Meva spent hours in the mornings fine-combing my head for lice and tending to all the sores on my body. First she would dab kerosene all over my scalp. Then she took the comb and loosened all the nits by digging into my skin. She scraped back and forth across my head until I bled. She would quickly remove the comb and attempt to kill the lice before they hopped out of reach and I could hear the click as she mangled each little louse-body between her finger and thumb. We would cheer, giggle and jump up and down feeling like victors. She would then allow me to play with her doll, for a short time, before repeating another round of the delousing. She would make a game out of it by saying, "Inka, how many cooties can we find this time?"

Next, Meva would tend to my body sores. She would use a soft cloth, dipped in disinfectant, to clean and swab each open sore. It was not as painful as the delousing, but it stung and itched. Meva then rubbed my body with salve to help ease the stinging and itching. But, it itched so badly that I would eventually scratch myself until I bled.

"Inka, if you don't scratch, I will let you play with my special dolls."

Even this offer couldn't prevent me from digging at myself.

After the evening delousing and disinfectant procedures, she would take me to my little room in the attic. There, she would make me kneel to say my prayers, tuck me into bed and kiss me good-night saying, "Dream of angels. They will always watch over you, Inka."

My pillow is damp with sticky, trickling blood. The bloody shapes scare me. I am too sleepy to care.

Turning my pillow over, I try to fall asleep before the dripping blood oozes all over this side.

I wonder if I might bleed to death before morning ...

In the morning my hair is dry with blood-encrusted masses stuck to the pillowcase and the back of my neck. This means Meva will need to wash and scrub my head before we can even begin our morning delousing.

These rituals luckily subsided in time and my sores and scalp healed. I was still a sickly child. My chest was always congested with phlegm due to undernourishment, lack of fresh air and my times in the cold, dank bunkers.

Since I was never allowed to go outside, Ciocia would go out on the attic balcony, on warm days, and place quilts and blankets over the railings to make it look as if she was airing them out. Then I was allowed to get a breath of fresh air on that balcony, but only if I sat on the floor. I was forbidden to stand or peek through the quilts and I was never to utter a sound.

It is night time. I see the big black sky filled with sparkling gold stars.

I stare at them one at a time until each star twinkles into many more. The whole sky lights up into a golden sleigh. It takes me to a place where I don't have to lie, or be scared or be **quiet**.

My eyes are sleepy.

I feel Meva scooping me up to take me back inside to my bed.

Tonight was so peaceful, not like other times when I sit on the balcony and can hear the distant rumbling of German planes letting us know it's time to scramble out of the attic and run down to the cellar.

I cuddle up with knees to my chin and hope to dream of my golden sleigh.

Our next door neighbors were Ukrainians and therefore presumed anti-Semitic. I was told I had to be especially careful about the neighbors whenever I sat out on my little balcony. One particular day I disobeyed (which was extremely unusual for me) and stood up to peek through the quilts hanging over the balcony railing.

I hear children playing outside. They are laughing and

running back and forth down there. I want to play with them. But I'm not supposed to be here. I must stay invisible. One tiny peek couldn't be so bad. I'll be so careful and quiet. I can stick my head between these two quilts just enough to watch them. Oh, it's a boy and a girl. They are older than me. They are running from tree to tree. I can't see them now. I'll just open these quilts a little more. If I stick my head out through the railing, just for a minute, I could see everything. Oops ... they're running this way and the boy is looking up at me. Oh, I need to go back inside, quick. I hope he didn't see me. Meva and Ciocia will be so mad at me. If he did see me, I hope it doesn't make the Germans come.

The nine-year-old boy **did** see my little blond head sticking out through the quilts. He told his parents what he had seen and since everyone knew there was no child at the Dobruckis, they scolded their son for making up stories and threatened to beat the shit out of him if he ever mentioned it again. That in itself was a miracle.

After that incident, Ciocia locked the door leading out to the balcony. I was confined to my little room and the big dark attic. Meva would bring me pencils and an occasional crayon and she taught me how to write and do simple math. I lost myself in drawing pictures, learning my ABC's and creating my fantasies with my friend-in-the-mirror. I would put on ten different outfits per day, look at myself in the mirror and talk to "me". The mirror was my friend and we had long conversations. It seems I was never lonely. I had a very loyal friend in the mirror.

I am tired of talking to my mirror friend.

Eddie, where are you? Show yourself in my mirror. Did the Germans kill you? I know they took you and your mommy and daddy and nanny. It doesn't matter if you're dead, Eddie, please come to my mirror and we can talk and play together. I know your nanny wasn't Jewish. Why did she go with you? You are my favorite cousin and I miss you. I'm sure my mommy misses her oldest sister, just like I miss you.

I would stand there scrunching my eyes and whisper-pleading at the mirror, but Eddie never appeared. Meva remembers that I spent hours and days just calling to Eddie in hopes that he would come to me and dress up and play with me. One day, while I was prancing around in one of the long gowns I tripped.

I see the top of the steps coming at me. I am rolling sideways down the steep stairs and getting all wrapped up in the long gown.

I can't see anything. I can't move my arms. Ouch, my head is banging against the cold, jagged steps. I must not cry out. I must not make a sound. Oh no, my body is smashing up against the kitchen door. Ciocia is going to be so angry with me.

Unbeknownst to me, a neighbor had dropped by to visit. When I smashed into the door, the hinges must have been loose because the entire door fell over and hit the neighbor. This neighbor actually passed out. Meva or Ciocia took me back up into the attic, put the door back on its hinges and told the neighbor that she suddenly passed out for no reason. The neighbor never questioned it.

♦ ♦ ♦

Life in the Dobrucki household seemed to revolve around me. If anybody got their hands on a piece of candy, Ciocia always said, "Any luxuries we get must always be saved for Inka."

The Dobruckis were very loving towards me. But Meva's brother, Janek, who was eighteen, played some weird games with me.

"Inka, come here I have a game we can play."

"Janek, why are you locking the door? Oh no, are we going to play the fart game, again?"

"Gottcha little Inka, bye-bye, I'll be back when the air clears."

He would leave me locked up in the room until I would hear Ciocia yelling at him, "Janek, you big lout, let the poor child out, and stop doing that to her!" He also had the boot game.

"Inka, come and help me get my boots off. Here, stand with your back to me and straddle my leg. Good. Now, grab onto the heel of my boot."

He could control whether the boot would slip off or not. He would then suddenly relax his foot so the boot would slip free. With the other foot he would push my rear end and send me flying across the room, landing up against the wall.

"That really hurts, Janek, and I don't like this game at all. I'm going to tell on you. After all I am only four years old."

When I ran to Ciocia and tattled, she grabbed Janek by the ear and smacked him across the back of his head yelling, "This is not how you treat a poor helpless child."

"Ouch, Momma, this poor helpless child is going to be the death of us all. We definitely have to get rid of her before she is discovered."

In truth, Janek spent little time at home, because he was very nervous and frightened that my presence was jeopardizing his entire family.

Yet, he was the one who often brought the chocolates home and always gave them to me. Even though I was so little and he was a bully, I think I had a crush on him. I learned how to aggravate him. Being the slowest eater in the world seemed to annoy him to no end. I ate breakfast until lunch, lunch until dinner, and dinner until I fell asleep in my plate. Most meals were eaten in the dining room and that meant I could stay downstairs in the house with the others. Janek felt extra jittery when I was downstairs too long.

I can remember how hungry I was when 'actions' took place. I was not allowed out of the attic during any of those times and I can still remember hearing dishes clanging downstairs. I presumed food was coming up but many times it didn't. On nights when bombs were part of the 'actions' and would explode very close to our house, they would allow me to come and stay downstairs. I would stick my head under a pillow and call to everyone,

"Get under my pillow with me. It's safe here."

For me, pillows were always a safe refuge in times of danger. At one point it became extremely dangerous, where even my pillow could not hide the noises or bright explosive lights. The bombs began to consistently loom over our house.

Mr. Buczynski, my mother's Ukrainian lawyer friend, would come by quite often and check to see if I was okay. During one of his usual visits, he gave the Dobruckis some disparaging news,

"I overheard someone talking about you and calling this a 'safe' house. They are saying that supposedly you are hiding a Jewish child. Due to this gossip, I have made arrangements with the cloister that takes in orphans and Jewish children. It is run by nuns and is a few short miles away from your house. It is imperative that you take Inka there, now – the sooner the better."

The very next night Uncle Dobrucki and I set off for

the cloister.

I know we are going someplace that has many other children. This sounds like fun.

Uncle says, "Come, Inka, I will carry you piggy back. We are going to walk through the woods tonight. Don't be scared. Everything will be just fine."

We were halfway there when a stray, sniper bullet came flying towards us. Suddenly, I feel horrible pain in my leg. I whisper

"Uncle, I think my leg is bleeding. It hurts so bad."

As Uncle stumbles to the ground he tells me, "I have an ouchy too and it is bleeding. We must turn around and go back to the house. We will try the trip again, after we get patched up, Inka."

The bullet grazed my leg. It went through the lower part of my calf, just above the ankle. Then it hit Uncle Dobrucki in the fleshy part of his hip, and exited. It did not strike any vital organs. When we got home, Ciocia cleaned our wounds with vodka and patched up Uncle with some sewing thread. I only needed a bandage.

The news the next morning, however, came as a major shock. The Germans knew that the cloister was hiding orphans and Jewish children. They attacked that particular night, bombing and killing every last soul in that cloister. Once again, I beat the odds.

♦ ♦ ♦

The Germans were trying hard to smoke out the rest of the Jews they thought might still be around. Once again the edict went out that every person whether sick, blind, or crippled was to appear in the city square at seven a.m. on a given day. The Dobruckis went crazy trying to figure out what to do. I've always thought that the sensible thing to have done would have been to hide me in the attic under a bundle of quilts. It would not have been a problem. Telling me not to make a sound would work because I already was well trained in maintaining a state of silence. But instead, they did the craziest thing – they laid me in the day bed that was in the dining room, in full view. I was only covered up to my chin with a warm quilt.

Ciocia and Meva hugged and kissed me, weeping, "Do not make a sound. Do not move. Lie here in bed until we come back. Don't be scared, Inka, we **will** be back."

They disappear and the door shuts.

What am I going to do all day? Just stare at the ceiling? I'll have to think up some ceiling games. Did she really mean it ... do not move ... lie here in bed until we come back ... I guess I can pee and poop here, in the bed. I wonder why? Who's going to feed me? I guess something bad is going to happen today. For now, I'll count the slats on the window covering ...

Suddenly I hear a horrendous noise, as if someone is trying to beat down the front door. And indeed they do kick it in. Two soldiers come into the house and start searching. They throw things around and break things as they move through the house. I hear glass breaking, dishes breaking and chairs being overturned. I just lay there staring at the ceiling. They finally walk into the dining room and I lay perfectly still. I only move my eyes.

The gun holsters are black and shiny. Are they going to shoot me? Their boots are bigger and blacker than I've ever seen. So, these must be the Germans. Now I know this is the reason I have been told to always stay invisible. I hope I can become invisible now. My heart is pounding. I'm afraid they will hear it. They are coming to the bed. I will close my eyes and float away. I can't even bury my head under a pillow. How can I stay safe?

All of a sudden I have a warm, wet feeling between my legs. I am really scared now. They are so close. I feel them jiggle the bed and now they are laughing.

Do they see me? Float away, float away to my beautiful place ... my princess place with lace and jewels and sugar plum trees ... and fairies and angels watching over me ...

There was a graduation picture of Uncle Dobrucki on the wall directly above the bed. Both soldiers stood right by my bed, looking and laughing at the picture. Their knees were touching the mattress and shaking the bed as they continued to laugh. With my eyes closed I was ready to feel a big arm grab me.

They are going to pull me out of my bed, drag me out of the house and kill me. They have stopped laughing. There is no sound. What are they doing? Have they noticed me? Are they pretending they don't see me? Through a tiny slit in one eye, I see their backs. Oh, I can hear their footsteps going out of the dining room. The door shuts. I will stay very still. They did not see me. I really can make myself invisible. I sure hope this means the family will come home soon. I am hungry and I don't want to poop in the bed. I have been lying here so quiet and for so long. I just want to scream.

A neighbor heard me howling, now and then, but was afraid to come out to quiet me. The family didn't return until ten that night. The poor Dobruckis, not knowing what had transpired at their house, didn't know what to expect. They feared the worst had happened; I had been discovered, and now they would be facing death.

Upon their return, they were so relieved to find that there were no soldiers around the house. They were dumbfounded at finding me still in the bed, untouched and alive. They kissed and hugged me all over. The joy of realizing that they would not be shot was great cause for celebration. They cleaned me up, set me at the dining table, let me eat whatever I wanted for as long as I wanted and listened as I told them my story of being invisible.

◆ ◆ ◆

I consider the encounter with the soldiers to be my most powerful miracle. At that point, my biggest gripe in life was the fact that Meva would not allow me to play with her "special" dolls.

Chapter Seven

Life In "The House"

In the Dobruckis' house there where two places of refuge for me in case of unexpected guests; one was under the baby grand piano in Meva's bedroom. There was a fireplace dividing it from the kitchen and the stairs to the attic. If they couldn't get me to the attic in time, they escorted and hid me under the baby grand piano. Ciocia used a huge hand-embroidered cover to hang down over the open sides of the piano. Unexpected company would come into the room while I was under the piano. At those times I knew I couldn't breathe audibly lest they hear me.

Grown-ups talk about the weirdest things and they scare themselves. They are talking about the war. They always talk about the war and Jews being killed. Didn't mommy say I am Jewish? That's why I'm not allowed to be seen. I can smell perfume. I can see a pair of sandals pacing back and forth. Oh, here comes a cough. I'll put my fist in my mouth and bite down, hard. The people are leaving the room and making a lot of noise. I can now explode with one quick, muffled cough.

The second hiding place was the unused salon, which in its day had been the formal living room. This room was never heated. At times it was well below zero because the solid wooden doors were always kept closed. Ciocia filled this room with lots of quilts and pillows. I would be hidden within the piles of pillows and quilts and any noise was muted by my dense, multi-layered igloo. However, I had contracted TB while in the ghetto, and my coughing spells were unpredictable and constant. So, when I had to cough I would stuff my mouth with corners of the quilts or parts of the pillows. It seemed that every time I was locked in the salon, that visitor was long winded and stayed forever.

I have a coloring book, today. I see a bag of raggedy material strips tucked between the folds of a quilt. I wonder what I could make. I know, I can make a doll out of strips of rags. I can play with my empty matchboxes and cotton balls to make little beds for my rag dolls. My igloo is dark. I'm tired of the dark, now. I think I'll crawl out. Oh, it's so icy cold out here. I know, Meva showed me how to push a tunnel-path toward the light. I miss my friend-in-the-mirror. I wish I was up in my attic. It is so much warmer there.

◆ ◆ ◆

My stay with the Dobruckis ended with me sitting at the window the day Momma came walking up the road to the house. When Ciocia said, "Inochka, this is your mother."

Apparently I said, "Oh, tomorrow another lady will come and you'll tell me that *she* is my mother."

Deep down inside, I knew she was my mother. Her coat, her smell, her touch and her kisses wiped away my doubt, my childish pout.

Momma looks so tired and thin. It feels so good to have her arms around me. I am not going to let her out of my sight. I'm going to keep on checking to make sure she stays in the house.

Now that she is here and I no longer have to sit and wait for her at the window, what am I going to do? She says she is tired and wants to sleep. I will stay with her while she sleeps.

My mother actually slept for three solid days. She had hitch-hiked all the way from Western Poland to where we were in the town of Czortkow. On her trip, she had stopped in a town that was about twenty minutes by car from Czortkow and quite by chance who does she suddenly see? A very familiar face; unbelievably it is Salo, her husband, my father.

My mother immediately runs up to him gasping, "Is Inochka alive?"

He heinously blurted out, "Frieda, I have been so busy, that I haven't had a chance to check."

"Salo, hardly any family consisting of a Jewish mother, father and child, are left alive. It is such a rare gift and yet you have no time to check to see if *your* child has survived the war or not? This war has warped your brain! How can a Jewish father abandon his only child?"

"I have other priorities now, Frieda, and here, let me show you a picture of my new love, Hanka."

He then whipped out a photograph of his latest floozy and asked my mother what she thought of this woman. My mother did not deign this remark worthy of an answer, and simply asked my father, "Could you please drive me to where Inka is?"

Even though he owned a car and he was now in a group that was reclaiming art and other valuable possessions that had been taken away from the Jews by the Germans, he made a bunch of lame excuses and retorted, "Maybe I could do it next week."

Completely disillusioned and yet determined to find me, mother ended up hitch-hiking; spending several hours, three different truck rides and an exhausting walk up the long road, to reach "the house" and find me alive.

◆ ◆ ◆

Why am I not having a much more powerful and explosive reaction to what I am experiencing on this return trip to my childhood past? Instead, I am sticking my head in the sand and retreating; reverting to my silent, invisible survivor mode. My attic behavior pattern of invisibility prevails. When I find out any bad news I tend to deal with it either in a soma-like trance or in a state of inconsequential babbling.

When my mind wanders, I begin to remember how it had been for my mother and me at the end of the war.

The war had ended eleven months sooner for us in the East. My mother had phony papers stating she was a Christian Polish woman, by the name of Yanina. Her last name was Buczynski. She ended up under German rule, for an extra eleven months due to an unfortunate happening, where someone tried to turn her in to the Gestapo.

A man, who worked in the same office as my mother, seemed to recognize her and confronted her with, "I know who you are. I know the names of your sisters and brothers. I even have information about other family members."

As much as my mother initially denied his inquisitions, and refused to admit that she was really Frieda Pearlmutter, she finally succumbed to his insistence and affirmed his suspicions. His true intention was to secure my mother's job for his wife. He used the admission to his own advantage and turned her in to the boss. The next day my mother's boss confronted her with,

"Andrew seems to think you are Jewish. If you indeed are Jewish, I would be happy to help you escape. I have a sister who lives on a farm in France. She would be receptive to having you stay there until the war ends."

When this accusation came out of the boss's mouth, my mother felt like she had just swallowed a gallon of ice-water. She felt sheer terror and yet she recomposed herself immediately saying, "This ridiculous accusation must be due to a bad case of mistaken identity. You don't need to bother your sister. I am staying right where I am. I have nothing to fear."

The next morning that office did not see her. She was gone. Instead of accepting her boss's offer, she fled westward to Krakow which remained under German rule for another eight months. I remember my mother saying to me,

"Why would Andrew do this to me? He was Jewish too."

Chapter Eight
Leaving "The House"

I lean in to see if I can feel Momma breathing. She has been sleeping for such a long time. I must stay here and keep watching to make sure she doesn't disappear. I have missed her so much. Her mouth is curled upward and is almost smiling. "Oh, Momma, you are happy to be here with me."

My excited voice rouses her. Her eyes flutter open and she reaches out and strokes my cheek before drifting back into a peaceful sleep. Snuggling up into her arms I feel totally safe and protected. I wonder *what is coming next.*

By the end of two weeks, Momma regains her strength. There is a lot of hushed talk, over my head, about how she spent *her* three years. I insist on cuddling into my mother's lap at every opportunity and pretend to sleep as she and Ciocia share stories of their near death experiences.

For the first time, Momma is hearing the 'miracle story' of the two German soldiers that came to our house and how they never harmed me. She seems to take it all in stride as she strokes me and squeezes me close to her and reminds Ciocia, "There have to be miracles along the way otherwise none of us will ever survive the aftermath of this war. Do you remember the time

I was across the street from the Warsaw Ghetto at the exact time that the Germans were dragging out the last of the Jewish bodies? It was a miracle that they never approached me, questioned me or stopped me to request papers, which I didn't have, at that moment. That was one of *my* miracles. I simply held my head high, and kept walking as if I belonged there."

As Ciocia and Momma continue on, I grow weary of trying to understand their interest in all these horrific tales. I am feeling restless and then Ciocia mentions **me.** I perk up to hear what she will say to Momma about me.

"Oh, Frieda, your little Inka is exceptional. There is nothing childish about her. How many three-year-olds can listen to demands, not argue, and remain silent for hours and days at a time. How a child can spend that much time alone with no complaints, is miraculous. She has always been able to keep herself entertained. Our biggest problem with Inka, is that she eats so slowly."

Guess they never caught on to why I made mealtime a game of 'how long can I make it last' so I can stay down here with them. Oh, now they're talking about Momma and me leaving.

"Frieda, will you and Salo be getting back together?"

"No, not after he showed me his disregard for Inochka. He had no interest in whether she was dead or alive. Ciocia, I can't believe that Salo has turned into such a heartless monster."

"So, Frieda, what will you and Inochka do, when you leave here?"

I can feel my throat tightening with fright.

What does she mean ... leaving here? This is where I live. Can't Momma and I stay here?

As I begin to stir, Momma strokes my head and cups her hands over my ears.

Two weeks later we packed up, left Czortkow and went to a city called Katowice. That's where my mother's sister had gone. My father, who was already quite wealthy because of his involvement with the reclaiming of Jewish goods the Germans had confiscated, was at least willing to find Momma and me a lovely big apartment in this new city. One of my mother's sisters, Pola, decided to move in with us with her husband, and Sylvia, their daughter.

Sylvia was that *second* child who had survived from

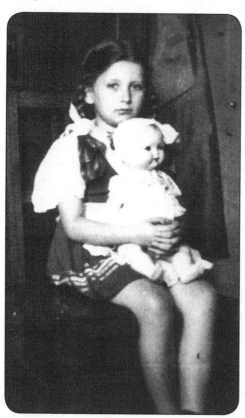

Czortkow. So they moved in with us and Pola totally took over. Oh boy, was she a witch. She acted as though the apartment was hers.

There were many very expensive Persian rugs in the apartment. My mother wanted to sell them to get money for food and Pola would not allow her to do so. We were there for three months only but we still had blackouts and one night Sylvia and I had broken a doll and decided it needed a funeral.

The doll that Sylvia and Inochka broke.

Raising the shades on the windows, without thought, and turning on the lights we proceed to perform our doll funeral. While burying the doll in a bottom drawer of an armoire we suddenly hear sirens and loud banging at the door. "It's the police, Inochka, they have seen our lights. Are they here to punish us or take us away?"

"Sylvia we're in trouble."

Men in uniform always brought feelings of terror and uncertainty. We crawled under the bed and held on to each other in sheer panic until Momma and Pola blew into the room in a rage to scold us. It took all our will power to keep straight faces and not burst into uncontrollable giggles.

Sylvia was one year older than I, almost to the day, and we felt like we were sisters. Until that time I had never really played with another child, nor had she. So we ended up having a very close bond promising each other never to lose touch, no matter what.

◆ ◆ ◆

I can only recall seeing my father twice during the time we lived in the apartment in Katowice. We never actually spoke or had any interactions with each other. During one of these visits he bursts through the front door and walks right past me as I am sitting on the toilet having terrible constipation and doesn't even see or look at me. He just hurries past the bathroom, takes off his jacket and hangs it on the back of a chair as he steps into the kitchen.

Oh, Daddy is here. I'd give anything to have him kiss and hug me, but he's too busy to notice me. If I lean forward and stretch my neck, I can see Momma and Tato (father) in the kitchen talking to each other from across the table. There's something sparkly sticking out of his jacket pocket. Is it something for me? Did he bring me a present? Does this mean that Daddy wants to live with us? Their voices sound cold and unfriendly. I don't think Daddy is going to stay. They are talking about money for Momma.

Momma says, "Just one of your diamond tiaras could more than adequately provide for Inochka and me until we reach the United States. They are so extravagant and filled with huge diamonds."

Solomon Hauser, 1946.

Now their voices are getting louder and Daddy just laughs at her.

"I do not intend or expect to reward you to such a generous extent."

Rising from the table, they are now shouting. Daddy grabs the jacket, tells Momma to sell the oriental rugs and turns to leave. Again, he walks right past me, as I am still on the potty. He never looks at me, or touches me or even says good bye.

For him, I do not exist. I feel invisible.

A month later, Momma and I are walking along the street and I spot my father in the crowd. I scamper up to him, hugging his leg. He gruffly peels me off with one swift smack and snarls at my mother, "Don't ever let her do that to me in public. No one here knows that I am married or that I have a child."

Frightened and hurt, I put my safe space between us, silently stepping behind Momma's skirt.

Daddy really doesn't like me and suddenly I don't think I like him, either.

"Salo, I cannot believe what I am seeing and hearing ... you are denying that you have a daughter ... and in front of her? You are still married and you do have a child! What you don't have is a conscience or a soul. I know I will still have to deal with you in the future, but at this moment, I can't stand the sight of you. We are definitely done!"

My hand and arm hurt as Momma yanks me in tow, dragging me away.

Will I ever see Daddy again?

I give him one more glance over my shoulder and I emotionally leave him, forever, standing there.

◆ ◆ ◆

While living in Katowice my mother plans our exit from Poland and attempts to get a divorce from my father. He explicitly refuses to cooperate. In his mind he did not want to be free to marry in the eyes of his numerous mistresses. Momma not only has to think about the two of us, but there is also Buczynski, the Ukrainian judge. Momma says it is our turn to keep him out of danger. He is now considered an enemy of the State.

When Buczynski procured phony papers for my father, he gave Salo his own name, Franciszek Buczynski. Now the new phony papers for Buczynski were in the name of Solomon Hauser. He was now posing as Frieda Hauser's husband.

My mother's goal was to get him safely out of Poland. Buczynski had a sister living somewhere in France and his goal was to reunite with her. We moved out of Katowice and went to Krakow to be closer to a viable railway system.

The three of us get another apartment in Krakow.

Momma and Buczynski have taken the only bedroom in our new apartment and I have to sleep on this day bed in the living room. I like the way the sun shines in through the windows.

Looking out, I watch the trolley-traffic clang by. This city is only partially bombed, and our street has sidewalks and trees. Nowhere do I see the usual mountains of fallen brick and rubble of bombed buildings as we had in Katowice. I feel safer. I can walk outside any time I want. I do not have to hide and Momma is with me.

When I turn seven years old Momma signs me up for piano and ballet lessons. On the corner where Momma and I catch the number-one trolley for the long ride to my piano teacher, there is the best ice-cream shop in the world. So I love going for my lessons because of the ice cream cone I get first.

In Krakow, 1947, Inka and her mother on the way to music lessons and a stop for ice cream.

I am sick most of the time while living in Krakow. I have continuous severe upper respiratory congestion due to my previous bout with Tuberculosis in the ghetto.

It's night-time now. I am coughing and I can't stop. It really hurts.

Momma gets up from her bed, and goes to her desk to get me some medicine. It is dark and I can tell she is fumbling to find the cough medicine that she keeps on her writing desk.

I wake up. It is morning. Momma is standing over me and gasps, "Inochka, your mouth is blue. Stick out your tongue. Oh, my God, your tongue is all navy blue. What is happening?"

Momma steps back and her expression changes from shock to sheer amusement, "Last night I was writing a letter and dipping my pen into the ink bottle. Later, when I heard you coughing I got up to give you the cough medicine. Since I did not want to turn on the light, I must have grabbed the ink bottle, thinking it was the medicine. But it seems to have stopped your cough."

A few days later I am, again, confined to my bed. I can barely breathe. Momma makes me a homemade mustard plaster. It is a combination of mustard seed, water and other herbs. She places the ingredients in an old, soft piece of cotton and sets it on my chest. It's an "old-wives" method used for decongestion. It smells sour and feels hot against my skin. As the concoction rankles and festers it becomes hotter and hotter. "Momma this is too hot."

"It will only take three minutes, Inka, relax. Before you know it Momma will take it off, so rest now, try to sleep."

We both doze off and awaken to my screams. My chest is on fire and burning my skin. "Oh Inka, we fell asleep and the mustard plaster has been on too long. Let me take it off."

She tries to lift it off but realizes that the cotton cover is stuck to my skin. She runs to get water soaked rags to try and soften the plaster and loosen it from my chest. As she lifts the plaster, parts of my skin peel off with it.

"Ouch, Momma! Oh look, I have bloody splotches all over me."

Through tears of panic she applies layers of Vaseline and bandages. Even though it relieves my congestion, the pain of the sores is much worse.

The next time I was sick with a respiratory ailment, Momma gave me yet another barbaric remedy. "This time Inka, I will not hurt you with a mustard plaster. We will use the Bainki method."

"What's a Bainki? Are you sure it won't hurt me Momma?"

"No, it will just pinch a little bit."

The Bainki remedy was the use of five or six clear glass orbs rinsed inside with alcohol and set on fire.

Momma comes at me with glass balls on fire. They are shaped like light bulbs without the necks and have an opening on the bottom. I am petrified.

"Momma, please don't set me on fire."

As she places one Bainki after another on my upper back, causing the flame to extinguish, a tight suction forms within the interior of each ball. "Ouch, this is much more than a pinch, Momma. No more, please, no more!"

"Inochka, be quiet and lay still. I'm almost done."

Each time the lit bulb grabs my skin and before the flame goes out the pin-prick pain makes me jerk and then leaves a brown ring on my skin. When Momma pulls the orbs off my back I am left with six giant brown polka-dots. Even though I look funny, and have some pain, this remedy is actually working. My cough stops for almost a whole week.

◆ ◆ ◆

At this time, food is still very scarce and terribly expensive. Momma is most concerned for my health and recovery so she once more turns to Salo for help. All she asks for is a bit of money to buy food. He promises to help. Two days later, early in the morning, his chauffeur arrives with "help." He hands my mother two or three broken typewriters and says, "Mr. Hauser[1] directed me to bring these machines to you. You are to sell them on the Black Market." Momma is stunned and very disappointed. She mumbles a few words of thanks and good-bye. However the chauffeur says, "Mr. Hauser said you would feed me breakfast."

On this day we have exactly one egg and two pieces of bread left. I watch Momma invite the chauffeur into our kitchen, seat him at our table and proceed to feed him that last egg and both pieces of bread.

Later, as an adult, I called my mother on this idiotic behavior and she said, "I was too embarrassed and proud to admit how desperate we were, to either the chauffeur or to Salo."

What a strange way to justify such a behavior.

But, Momma did manage to sell the broken typewriters, and secure enough food for at least another week. Buczynski still had no means to earn anything. He was still considered an enemy to the State.

The biggest thing I do recall about our lives in this apartment was the drastic change in Buczynski's behavior. He went from being a kind, gentle, helpful suitor towards my mother to becoming unpredictable, angry and dangerous. He thought he and Momma would marry. But my mother felt she would be a prisoner, under his rule, and I had often told her I would run away if she stayed with him.

---

1. At this time, Isabelle's father was using the assumed name Franciszek Hauser.

One day I saw him running after my mother with a hatchet in his hand. He had discovered that she was seeing another man. My mother locked herself in her bedroom and I was cowering in the shadows of the living room. He took the ax and put it through a panel of the door. She screamed, "Stop it, stop it, Franciszek. You have gone totally mad!"

Her crying and yelling brought him back to the reality of the moment. He pulled the ax out of the door, dropped it and stormed out of the house. When he returned he was subdued and actually never touched or hurt either one of us.

I became deathly afraid of Buczynski and the best part of my day was when he went out for his afternoon walk by the river. Those were my two hours of freedom each day. Even though I thought he was the weirdest person I had ever known, and I did not trust him, he was my "Tiger Mom." He kept me busy and involved in various educational endeavors. At age six, I was able to read the equivalent of the New York Times. Many years later, somewhere between 1967 and 1970, Buczynski wrote me a letter stating that Washington D.C. was aiming laser beams directly at his house in France and would I be good enough to contact Washington and make the situation stop. My half-brother Joel went to France and met him. Joel reported back that he was completely out of touch with reality and seriously deranged.

◆ ◆ ◆

After we left Krakow, I remember us taking many trains on our journey to get out of Poland. Buczynski was still with us, but I don't remember his presence. The first few trains were so badly crowded that I recall sitting on top of people. My mother was lucky just to have a spot to stand and sometimes to even sit.

Mamusiu (Momma) holds me to her chest. Strange bodies are leaning against us. I can hardly breathe. We are packed so tightly in this hot, smelly sardine-can train car. A man needs to move because his leg is crushed. Several others must change positions so that he can straighten his leg. A very handsome, strong, young man, who is most anxious to help my mother in any way he can, grabs me and lifts me above his head so that all the others can shift. As he hands me back to Momma, I really need to pee and I squeeze my popo as hard as I can. "Momma, I really have to pee. What do I do now?"

"Just let it go, Inochka, we have no choice. Here, stand between my legs at the edge of the seat."

"But it will get my panties and my dress all wet, Momma."

"We cannot get to the bathroom. Just spread your legs and let it hit the floor. I will change you the next time the train stops."

I am trying to hold it in, but it starts to leak out. The warm liquid begins to trickle into my panties. It is so warm and I can't stop it from gushing. It actually feels good to let it out and I look around to see if anyone is watching me. Momma looks away so I won't feel embarrassed. It runs down the inside of my thighs as it dribbles out of my panties and onto the wooden planks. I am feeling sooo much better and I lean back against Momma and suddenly feel very sleepy. I do not know where we started this trip or where we are going. Somewhere along the way we were separated from Buczynski.

I do remember when we started riding in cattle car trains to try to get out of Poland. My worst fears were from **those** trains. My mother had one big black suitcase that held the few necessary personal items, small pieces of silver and precious stones. This suitcase also served as my bed. It contained a small pillow and a down quilt and it held a special container that we could use as a toilet.

There are no seats in this train. I am glad I have my suitcase-bed to sit and sleep in. There is plenty of space and I can move around and Momma passes the time by telling me stories of her childhood ... the train is stopping. I wonder if we are in a station or just out in the middle of some empty field. It's a station. Momma is scrambling around in the bottom of the suitcase and pulls out several solid silver forks. Oh no, Momma is going to leave me here, again.

"Don't move. Don't talk to anybody. Stay put and I will be back. I promise."

As Momma jumps off the train my stomach knots up in fear and yet I know that when she returns we will have something to eat. I am so glad I have my quilt to wrap around me until I see her coming back. I know she is going into the station to "handle" a deal with the black marketeers.

Oh, the train is starting to hiss ... it is too soon to be leaving ... and Momma is nowhere in sight.

Stepping out of my suitcase, I run to the open doors and holding on to the door jamb, I lean out and shout out ... "Momma the train is leaving. Where are you?" Now I can see her bursting out of the train station, jumping across sets of tracks and running towards me just in time to grab hold and hoist herself up into our car as the train begins to move.

"Inochka, we did great today. Look, we have bread and ham and cheese. Let's have a party."

"No, Momma, I am still so scared that I might never

have seen you again. What if you hadn't caught the train? What would have happened to me?"

"In order to be rewarded in one way, one has to pay the price on the other. I am here now, that's all that matters, but if it ever does happen that I miss the train, always get off at the next station. I will find you. Come, let's eat."

We survived all the way to Austria in this manner, and thinking the worst was over, we had no idea what lay ahead.

◆ ◆ ◆

Since we have no money when we arrive in Austria our only choice is to go by trucks to a DP (Displaced Persons) Camp. The name of the camp is Klineminchen. This camp is a small converted concentration camp. I remember they take all the children in one truck and all the adults in another. Again, I am petrified.

How am I going to find my mother in this huge place?

Our truck comes to a stop in front of a huge camp dining hall. Burly men are reaching up to help each one of us off the back of the truck. I look into the eyes of a sweaty, red-faced young man and wonder if I can trust him. As I hesitate, he smiles and says, "Sweetheart, you will be reunited with your mom in just a short while. Here, let me help you down." He slowly extends his arms and I let myself believe that this is the truth. I follow the line of children into the dining hall. It is sheer chaos inside. Children and adults are racing around, frantically searching for their own.

Oh, Momma, where are you? There are so many blond mommies running this way and that. I feel so small and can't see the faces. I am so afraid I won't find you.

"Inochka, I'm over here. Inochkaaaaa, turn around."

Turning, I see Momma pushing her way through the mass of searching parents and I run into her arms. All of us children eventually find our parents and a semblance of order falls over the hall. We are then taken to our living quarters. It is a very large room which has to be shared with about 30 people. The beds are bunk beds and my mother puts a blanket around my bed so I will not see the young adults fornicating. According to my mother the conditions in this camp seem to be as bad as the ghettos in Poland. After such a war, it caused young people to lose all sense of shame or control or caring.

The next day we surprisingly run into a first-cousin of my mother's whose name is Sally Pearlmutter. She is all of thirteen or fourteen years old, traveling with one other teenager, and if I think I have a sad tale to tell, this poor child has a story way above and beyond anything I could even imagine.

She was eight or nine years old when the war had begun. She walked into her home one day to find her entire family sitting at the dining room table – dead. She ended up living all alone in cemeteries. Eventually she was found and placed on one of the death trains. When you are meant to live – you just do. She just happened to be on a train where someone was able to disconnect several of the last few cars. Sally, along with several others, was able to escape and I don't know how she survived the rest of the war. But here she was in the DP camp with us.

As Momma and I settle into the DP camp routine, we discover we must also procure our own necessities for food, and sanitary hygiene. The only way to get served in the soup-line is to have your own container. Behind the dining room there was a big mound of dirt with bits of garbage and pieces of shiny metal. I cleverly start digging to see if I can uncover any eating utensils and that's when I meet my large Donald Duck orange juice can. I now have my very own soup holder.

I do not mind the taste of the grey slop they are ladling into my can. Momma cannot stomach this stuff. According to her, even hungry pigs would not eat this slop.

Today they have only filled my container half-way up. I will find a comfortable spot, maybe under a tree.

I place the can between my legs and enjoy every last drop of the sludge.

I have met several other children at this camp who are mostly Hungarian. Within a week or two I am somehow communicating with these kids in their own language. I am having a wonderful time here. One day we decide to build a see-saw. We are able to find one long old plank and a saw-horse. We proceed to build the see-saw by nailing the plank to the middle of the saw-horse. When we are done, at least four kids can sit on each side of the board. It works really well until the whole thing snaps in half and we all fall off.

Ouch ... Ugh ... my arm hurts. Why is my arm pointing in such a strange direction? Momma is running towards me.

"This is just what I need now, a possible broken arm."

"I'm so sorry Momma and it was all my idea to build this silly see-saw."

At first Momma rushes me over to the camp infirmary. The nurse in charge states that my arm is definitely broken and I must be taken to a doctor. She immediately calls a camp director who takes us into town to see a doctor. I come out with my arm in a snow-white cast and I can hardly wait to show it off to the other children.

Going to town turned out to be a very important trip. While Momma was sitting in the waiting room filling out paperwork with the receptionist she made a shocking discovery.

"I see your last name is Hauser. I just recently met a man named Hauser. Do you know him? Are you related to him?"

"Yes, he is my child's father and my husband **and** I have been trying to find him."

"Oh my, I understand that he lives in a gorgeous villa with a woman. Would that be his sister?"

Without saying yes or no they look at one another, knowingly and without any hesitation the receptionist hands Momma his address.

The next week, armed with his address, Momma and I go to Vienna to face my father. We arrive at his house and it is a virtual palace, as far as I am concerned. Two huge lion statues grace the entry, one on each side of the front door. They stand guard as we approach the beautiful two-story structure. We ring the bell and a lady, dressed in a maid's outfit, answers the door. Luckily my mother can speak German fluently so she tells the woman who we are. Inside the entryway there is a picture of my father on the table. I point and shout, "Tato ... Father!"

The maid grabs her head between her hands and says in German, as she leads us into the grand salon, "*Ah, ach du liebe* – I had no idea he had a child and a wife."

She is a bit confused and asks us, "Who is Hanka then?"

My mother replies, "She is Salo's mistress."

All of a sudden my father enters and upon seeing us, a look of agitated suspicion crosses his face. He grabs my mother's arm and ushers her into another room to talk. The maid nervously ushers me into the kitchen and plies me with every delicacy imaginable. After being used to the slop from the DP camp, my taste buds explode in delight with all this food. Even though we are in the kitchen I am aware of my mother's voice begging my father to let us move in for just a few days, or maybe a week. My mother tells him she is making plans with a Polish underground group to sneak across the Alps from the Austrian border into Italy. My father spits back, "Regretfully, this will not work, because my mistress would be uncomfortable having you here."

Having eaten all of the goodies I could stuff into my little stomach, I leave the kitchen and head for the salon. As I enter the hallway I see a woman coming down the stairs in a very sheer negligee. It was so sheer that my mother races over to me and shields my eyes. There is no repartee between the woman, Hanka, and my mother. Turning to me, Momma says, "I must convince your father to let us stay here, Hanka or no Hanka. I have to get us out of that hell-hole DP camp."

My mother turns and walks right past Hanka as if she were not there. She drags me back with her to face Salo again, describing what it is like inside the DP camp, for us. "Salo, there is a stream that runs through the middle of the camp and often we see feces and human bones floating in the water. One day the children were playing and digging near the stream and they uncovered a burial pit and began playing with the human bones. Is that what you think your child should be playing with?"

She pauses briefly to strengthen her plea and begins again. "The bathroom, with its putrid stench is one long room with a narrow slat sporting ten holes carved in it.

It's a communal shit-house. There is no water to flush. It's simply an outhouse. Inochka is petrified of using this outhouse. The holes are way bigger than her little tush and she's terrified of falling in."

Father replies, "That is really a crying shame. The conditions sound terrible, but the decision is firm. You are not staying here."

As my mother realizes there is no chance that Salo will act humanely and allow us to stay, she says, "Someday you will need something in kind from us and we will be sure to remember your actions, here, today."

She wished him the best of luck with Hanka (who later committed suicide). As we were leaving, my mother muttered, "I can understand him treating me, the wife, this way but his own daughter – his own flesh and blood? The war years have obviously scrambled his brain." As we left, defeated, his maid came running after us with a huge package of food. His cellar was stocked with every delicacy you could think of; cheeses and salami, to jellies and jams, and candy and caviar. It never occurred to him to share with us yet his maid, a perfect stranger to us, was heartbroken and gave us everything she could throw together in a moment's notice.

♦ ♦ ♦

My father was taking a big chance with his negative reactions because at this stage many different police agencies, from various cities, were after him. He had sold an American Care ship (from the USA with food and supplies) to some gullible, stupid person. The ship was not his to sell. And yet he made millions of Marks on this scam and therefore was able to live in style.

In later years, I always told my mother what a fool she was for not exposing him and turning him in to the authorities. She would forever repeat, "I just couldn't do it. Yes, I was an idiot. But I couldn't do it to him. However, years later, I *was* able to return his kindness for turning us out the way he did. I made it impossible for Salo to remarry into a very wealthy family by informing them that he had a child whom he had deserted. He was stupid enough to give me that family's address rather than his own. So, I wrote a letter to Salo and sent it to this family's address stating ... 'he needs to take care of old business before embarking on a new life.' That was enough for his bride-to-be to realize what sort of person he was. It was her money, not her, that interested him."

◆ ◆ ◆

In the following days and weeks my mother continued to connect with an underground, Polish (non-Jewish) group who was going to cross the Alps into Italy. She made arrangements for all three of us (mother, me and Buczynski, who had reconnected with us) to join them. When my mother began dealing with these people, at first they refused to let her join because of me. They told us many adults weren't able to survive such a trip, let alone a young child. The rarity of even seeing a child, in connection with this group, was apparent. But my mother shared with them all the traumas I had already been through from age three to six and how well I was able to conform. It would be second nature for me to survive and be silent.

On a designated night a car picks us up and drives us to an isolated field where a huge potato-transport truck was waiting for us. We join the group of about fifteen other people and wait.

It is so cold and dark tonight. My feet are frozen.

A Polish adjutant whispers, "Climb into the back

of the truck and hide behind the sacked potatoes. Stay quiet. We will be driving through several check-points. We will let everybody out at the Austrian border. Then we will meet up with you on the Italian side. Don't even think about hiding inside a potato sack to have a free ride rather than walking across the border."

I don't want to let go of Momma's hand but Buczynski is lifting me up into a tunnel of black. These bags feel rough and lumpy and cold.

We are crammed and stuck in the back bowels of the truck-bed.

People are whispering. They are scared. Who are we scared of? Why is this ride such a secret? Why are we not allowed to go from one place to another? I thought the war was over.

After a fast, bumpy, uncomfortable ride the truck stops. We all quickly climb out in silence. The rest of our trip must be on foot. We begin our escape across the Alps.

The feel of the snow on my bare, sandaled feet is needle-sharp. I shiver in my light spring coat and grab for Momma's hand. But Buczynski quietly and firmly takes my hand and says, "Hang on tight. Don't let go. The ground is very uneven and the trail over the mountain will be narrow and steep."

I know Momma is right behind us. I cannot see or hear her. The crunch of my footsteps in the snow and the thump, thumping of my heart fill my ears. I must keep up.

I suddenly lose ground. I am too close to the edge of the mountain path and I feel myself slipping sideways away from Buczynski. Our hand-grasp tightens and my free arm grabs onto his jacket. I am in mid-air and suddenly one of my sandals falls off my frozen foot. It rolls over the edge and bounces down the mountain side. It starts a small avalanche and the next thing we know, bright lights appear from the road below.

"Everyone hit the ground. Don't make a sound."

Blasting gunshots surround us. Why? Is it the Communists? We lay there motionless in the freezing snow until the lights vanish, the shooting stops, and it seems that all is clear.

*I must not make any more problems for the group. Oh, my body aches and I cannot feel my fingers and toes. Am I in a scary dream? Wake up, wake up, get out of this ... I can't ... this **is** real.*

When it seems safe we resume our journey and walk all night. My feet are numb and painful from the cold. When my shoe-less foot begins to turn purple, Buczynski lifts me up and carries me the rest of the way. Somewhere towards dawn, we reach a Red-Cross hut on the Italian side. They give us food and drink. Once again we are put into the potato truck.

This time I do not have to hide.

The British are now manning the truck. I am the "little belle of the ball" with the soldiers. They cannot believe that a child of six could have just accomplished the task of crossing the Alps. The trucks take us to a little town called Predapio. We remain in this DP camp for several days. It is much better than any of the other DP camps. But, I have never experienced such heat in my life. I eat watermelon all day long to stay hydrated. It feels like it is 110 degrees during the day. From Predapio we somehow find transportation to Rome. Once in Rome we are finally able to put Buczynski on a train to Paris.

Yeah, freedom at last! I will never get involved with anyone who speaks Sanskrit. This man was so weird, so strict, and so insane! Now he is gone!

◆ ◆ ◆

Once in Rome, my mother found a furnished room with a family named Vallone. It was located on a street called Via Nazionale. (On a recent trip to Rome, I found the building. Absolutely nothing had changed in all the years other than now it was a rooming house without the original family.) The Vallones were a close-knit happy family consisting of a mother, a father, and a thirteen-year-old daughter, Gracia Maria. She had long braids and the thickest glasses I had ever seen. There was also a nephew, Tami, who was much closer to my age of seven and a blind grandmother. I had my first lesbian experience when Gracia Maria took me into the bathroom with her one day and told me to suck on her boobs, which I did. Then she returned the favor by sucking on my non-existent boobs. Then I had my first heterosexual involvement with her cousin Tami. We decided to play the "you show me yours, I'll show you mine" game. Except that we did it in front of the blind grandmother. We were in Grandma's room, inside her armoire. Grandma, at one point, shuffled into her room and we had to be extremely quiet so as not to be discovered. Tami showed me his little "gold eggs" but I finked out on him and slipped out of the armoire and tip-toed out of the room without Grandma's suspicion.

I lived in this furnished room with my mother for only a short time. She found a Polish group that formed

Inka and her mother in Rome.

a summer camp somewhere in the countryside outside Rome. The people in this group were mainly married couples with one or two children and a sizable group of young adults. This group was simply Polish. My mother signed me up for about a month since Rome is hot and muggy and sticky in the summer time. This was a delightfully cool, mountain resort. All of the children under age 15 were there with their parents. I was the only eight-year-old there all by myself. My mother dropped me off, and simply asked some of the other mothers if they could keep an eye on me. It was actually a very pleasant place for me and the fact that I had no parents, the familiar feeling of surrealistic freedom came over me again.

One day I was chased by a bull. I jumped a four-foot wall, smack into a chicken coop, and the hens ran after me, pecking at my feet. Being petrified I felt the need to take a dump. By the time I made it to a bathroom it was too late. My sun suit was filled. I took it off and washed it out in the toilet, all the time crying my heart out that I had no mother to go to for help. Here I was, having to do things, again, for myself and at such an early age. I put the wet sun-suit back on, and went back to my room to change.

My mother was able to secure an extremely high paying job as a bookkeeper for HIAS, a Jewish Organization that reeducated Jewish immigrants for employment status. How she talked her way into that job is beyond me as she had never had any prior office experience. She had signed me up for public school as a second grader. But she was very nervous about me walking to and from school alone and being on my own most of the day while she was away at work. So, she checked into boarding schools in the area and was told that the best school was a convent called Santa Dorotea (St. Dorothy's).

After being cooped up in an attic for three years, going through the horror of the train rides, and experiencing the crossing of the Alps, life for me just seemed like a wonderful, surrealistic fantasy. That wonderful feeling did not last for very long.

Chapter Nine

The Convent

It doesn't matter how I feel about this sudden decision. I just follow Momma and obey her. The bus comes to a stop in front of a huge, cold, spooky looking red-brick building. Shivers of fear envelop my body. The bus ride has left me feeling sick to my stomach. Grasping Momma's hand we step down from the bus and I recoil.

"This is a wonderful school, Inka, you will be well taken care of here. You will make new friends and learn how to be a lady with proper manners."

"I don't care, Momma, I just want to stay with you. Please don't leave me here."

Momma doesn't appear to hear my pleas and proceeds to walk us up to the enormous carved, wooden front doors. Pushing the bell and waiting, I feel my stomach begin to tighten and it sends a surge of nausea upward. Leaning over to miss my shoes, vomit shoots out all over the sidewalk and Momma shrieks,

"Inochka, get a hold of yourself. Stop this behavior, immediately. We *are* going to get you in here."

Glancing up at her, I catch the distortion of her rigid face. It has lost its sweet mien and has been replaced with her tense muscle-twitching, tooth-grinding, purse-lipped icy stare. Momma's eyes peering sideways at me stab through my entire being.

It's not her words I listen to, but the "look" she gives me. I know this look all too well and once it appears I am helpless to dispute any of her wishes and silently resume my obedience.

Pulling out a hanky and spitting on it Momma gently wipes around my mouth and pushes back the wisps of hair as the door begins to creek open.

"*Bon giorno, Seniora i Signiorina. Io sono Antonio.*"

My mouth drops open as this strange, age-less man lisps a welcome to enter. Momma, in fluent Italian replies, "We are here for an appointment with Madre Generale."

Crossing the large, open, plant-filled atrium we are confronted with another gigantic closed door. Antonio opens it and we enter the large, tiled waiting room. It is lined with ancient, carved wooden benches shoved up against the walls which are covered with immense oil paintings of various nuns. Antonio gestures for us to sit and says in his lisping Italian, "I will inform Mother Superior that you are here."

"Inochka, do not say anything about being Jewish. You are now a Polish, Catholic young lady. Do not tell your new little friends or any of the nuns. Let me do all the talking."

"Yes, Momma, whatever you say. You're not leaving me here today, are you?"

"No, today is just for the interview."

If I act badly, maybe they won't want me. But I know I must listen to and obey Momma. Maybe I will find another girl, like my cousin Sylvia, and we can be friends. Maybe they will have some dolls here and ...

A panel in the wall opens and a tall, beautiful, kind

looking woman dressed in a flowing, black, full-length gown glides toward us. Her face is framed in a stiff, white, honeycombed headdress showing off her high cheek bones, aquiline nose and full-lashed, dark-lined, blue eyes. Her kind face brings comfort to my nervous stomach and I relax.

"Hello, Isabella and Seniora Hauser, welcome to our school. I understand that you are interested in having Isabella board here. May I ask why?"

"I have been told by my Italian friends that this school has the best reputation in Rome for being a top finishing school for young girls. Not only will my Inka get an excellent education but she will also be taught how to knit, crochet, petit point, play piano and become knowledgeable in the Arts ..."

As Momma and Madre continue the interview process I learn that many of the girls at this convent are from Italian-born families of noble birth. The war has left many of these families in financial ruin. Therefore, several of these "noble" girls have left and now there are openings for students with money. When Madre learns that I am fluent in Italian and enrolled in piano and ballet lessons, her demeanor begins to reflect that I will be accepted here.

By the end of the interview I know my fate is sealed. Within two weeks I am officially enrolled and my time with Momma comes to yet another end.

♦ ♦ ♦

I immediately dislike this place. The first morning I wake up in a four poster bed before anyone else is awake.

Everything seems so grey and cruel looking. The walls are grey, the floors are grey. Even the air is ugly grey. It's so strange here. I can't go anywhere on my own. We have to do everything group style for each and every minute of the day. I need to go to the bathroom. Do I dare get up and go on my own?

It is so very regulated and strict. Always knowing I must "obey," I hold it in until the lights are clicked on and we all march into the bathroom for our daily hygiene routine.

"Girls, hurry now, use the toilet, brush your teeth, wash your faces, get your combs and cologne and line up to have your hair sprayed and then you will do your sponge bath."

The real bath and a shampoo only happen once a month.

My turn is coming. The girls in front of me are wincing. Why? Now it's my turn. The fine comb is scraping my scalp just like when Meva used to pick at my nit infested head. Oh no, do they have those nasty nits here, too? It turns out this is just for prevention.

Each day consists of rising at six a.m. and going to Chapel before breakfast. After breakfast we all line up in front of the dining hall to get our daily spoonful of cod liver oil. There are two nuns dispensing the oil. They use only two spoons to service approximately sixty girls. (Then they wonder why we have outbreaks of certain diseases and maladies.) Then it is back to Chapel. It is the same for each meal ... before and after every meal ... Chapel. In the mornings we go to class. In the afternoons it is back to class until five p.m. then on to pre-dinner Chapel.

Dressed in this silly uniform I look like something straight out of the olden days. This navy blue dress, with all its pleats from the waist down, with the big, white dickie-collar and long sleeves makes me feel overstuffed. The scratchy stockings with high-top shoes give me hives.

Once in a blue moon we are taken to a nearby park. On these occasions we are made to wear hats. They are the big-brimmed navy-blue hats with the bows hanging down the back. We definitely look like something from another century ... just like little Madeline in the books.

The nuns are extremely mean and nasty. They never seem to give us compliments but whenever they reprimand us which is *most* of the time, they think we can't hear them unless we are yanked by the ear.

I'm going to get cauliflower ears if they don't stop pulling them. The only nice nun is Madre Generale (Mother Superior). She is so pretty and kind. Why did she join the convent and become a nun? Most of these nuns are very plain looking to downright ugly. I am so-ever-wanting to crawl back into my quiet, solitary little attic with my mirror-self. I am going to do things to cause myself trouble. This is really very unlike me ... I always obey ... I always do what I am told. Now it is time to rebel.

Running up and down the stairs my leather bottom soles smack in a staccato statement of rebellion. I get into trouble. In the dining room, lunch includes a dish containing green peppers. I eat everything on my plate except the green peppers. The nun in charge of serving us decides to make a big deal out of my uneaten peppers. I simply say, "I don't like the taste. I am not going to eat them." I get into trouble.

For dinner that night I am served a large, boiled green pepper and nothing else.

If they think this is going to make me change my mind it won't. It's not my mind ... it's my taste buds. Just the smell of this green pepper is making me gag and choke.

So, I go to sleep on an empty stomach. For the next day or two I am served one large green pepper at every meal.

Here it comes again. I am so hungry but I just can't. Oh no, here come the kitchen nuns. Their mean and determined expressions are frightening. Why are they surrounding me? Help! Four hands are too much for me to fight back. The pepper is touching my lips. The smell is too much ...

Forcing me to eat it, I immediately vomit repeatedly and cannot stop. I lose consciousness. When I wake up, I think I'm dead and in heaven. I am staring at little cherubic angels, white puffy clouds and a blue sky.

I'm not dead... I am in the infirmary. I am in trouble again.

Over and over I create havoc. And yet my most serious infraction unexpectedly brings me back into good graces with the convent.

Our sleeping quarters have somewhere between ten to fifteen girls in the same large dormitory style room. Each girl has her own four-poster bed. The bed is totally enclosed by heavy drapery around all four sides. As we undress for the night, the drapes are supposed to be fully closed so that not even an ankle is exposed.

I really want to feel the freedom of nakedness.

"Girls, open up your drapes. Take all your clothes off

and let's sing and dance around our beds. Look how high I can jump up and down on my bed. This is fun."

I feel a sense of "freedom" again ... my wonderful surrealistic fantasy feeling. Standing in the middle of my bed, stark naked, with the drapes wide open I watch as one by one the other drapes begin to slowly, tentatively, open as each girl peers out to see what I am doing. "Let's all do this! It's fun!"

When the last drape opens and we are using our beds as trampolines I insist on more. "Take off your PJ's and let's dance naked." They do. We are all squealing with joy and laughter as we jump off our beds and scatter about the room in wild abandonment. Singing the latest hymn from our repertoire of Godly gospels, we escalate to a level of pure pandemonium. Suddenly, we come face to face with an irate, red-faced nun. There she stands, clothed only in a plain white flowing gown, her head bare and donning nothing but a crew-cut. To me she looks like a white ghost. Fright grips us all. This time I am in major trouble.

Most of the girls scamper back to their beds. A few of us remain still and stand frozen like deer caught in on-coming headlights. "This must be Isabella's doing," scoffs the nun as she grabs me by the ear, orders me to put my on PJ's, and literally drags me by the ear out the door and down the hall. I end up in Madre Generale's office, the one person in this convent whom I like and admire.

Now I have really messed up. I am ashamed. Madre Generale is disappointed and I can see the hurt in her eyes. She is not going to let me off this time. I can tell I am about to receive a very stringent punishment.

"Isabella, this evening you will go back to Chapel and

kneel for one hour on a bag filled with hard, pointy corn kernels and you will pray for forgiveness."

"Yes, Madre Generale."

This really hurts. These corn kernels are poking through my stockings and piercing my knee caps. Nobody else is in here. Hmmm, if I push the corn-kernel bags to the back of my knees, I can last the hour of kneeling. Oh, that's much better. I feel a cough coming ...TB? Or not TB ... Consumption be done about it? Of cough, of cough! It is not the cough you cough in. It is the coffin they carry you off in ...

I am getting really sleepy and bored. Why is the altar wavy? The statue of Mary just moved. I know it did! Statues don't move! Hmmm, I am well-versed in lying. I know. I can make a big deal out of the possibility that the Virgin Mary moved.

I ran screaming, out of the Chapel, and bumped into a group of nuns. I told them about my spiritual miracle. "Mary beckoned to me. She moved. Mary moved. She reached out and touched my heart and filled my mind with goodness!"

The nuns actually believed me and took me straight to Madre Generale. I described this miracle to her in non-stop, over-dramatic displays of convincing improbabilities and to this day I presume that she also believed me because the next day, in the dining room, she stood me up on her platform.

"Girls, our Isabella had a miraculous happening last night. While praying for forgiveness for leading her group into immoral and sinful behaviors, she saw the Virgin Mary beckon to her. This has made our Isabella realize the errors of her ways and has astonishingly absolved her of her evil ways. In all my years as your Madre Generale, this intense appearance of the Virgin

Mary with one of our own is truly a blessing for us all. Everyone, please show our Isabella your respect."

Even I began to believe my own fabrication and to wonder if I was a "chosen" one because of having survived my childhood in Poland. From then on the other girls seemed scared of me and kept their distance. I liked it that way.

I really never had or found a close friend while I was at this convent. I never had to eat another green pepper and I was given many privileges that I did not deserve. I became an anomaly.

Every Christmas the convent put on a play and I always had the role of the angel because I was blond. In Italy cherubs and angels were commonly depicted as blond. There was only one other blond child, Serenella. She had a terrible speech impediment and so I was always the chosen one.

These wings are huge and heavy. They are tied onto my body so tightly. I can't breathe. But ... Hah! The Jewish kid gets the top billing.

Each year girls turning eight qualified for their first communion. It was a big to-do in the convent with many other dignitaries invited.

The day of the Sacrament finally arrived and we had no breakfast because we were not allowed to eat anything before taking communion. As our procession entered, rose petals were strewn along the aisle leading to the altar.

I just love my full-length white velvet gown. My little white veil is so soft and lacy. My patent leather Mary Jane shoes match perfectly. I am so excited. I don't care that I am going to be receiving the Lord's body. I just want to show off my beautiful clothes.

In order to receive communion one had to go to confession. Often I could not think of any transgressions so I would make up and confess stories that were total lies. Therefore, the following week, I could confess that I had lied. It all seemed fair to me.

Even from age eight, I was a total Agnostic. I only wanted to play the game. Although I had little use for religion, the only sacred rite I wanted was the act of communion. I totally believed that the wafer was alive. It was the only thing I really took seriously within my religious experiences.

Here comes the priest. My turn is coming. I finally get to receive my first ... why are my ears ringing? Whoa, there are a million little pin-prick stars all around me ...

I passed out right at the altar and had to be carried off to a side room. When I came to, my mother and the Vallone family were standing over me. So, that day was not to be my first communion but I got a party anyway.

Inka's first communion – with the Vallone family, 1947. Inka is in the white dress.

My mother had invited the Vallone family of six to the communion ceremony since mother was still renting their furnished room. We all went back to the rooming house for my party. As a gift they presented me with the most beautiful ivory covered Missile. They also gave me a gorgeous little veil and white gloves. It was the first time I ever received real "gifts."

◆ ◆ ◆

Every Sunday was visiting day at the convent but we could never leave the school to go home for a weekend. My mother was sure to come every Sunday except the *one* Sunday that we had a recital and I was chosen to play the piano.

Where is Momma? Here I sit in my new emerald-green ruffled dress. I feel like a frog. My piano recital piece is all about a frog. It is time for me to perform. I am so upset. Momma is not going to hear or see me, today. The show must go on ...

The following Sunday she came to see me but brought a man with her. I felt instant distrust and dislike towards this man. My initial reaction was right. He turned out to be Joachim Lustig, who later would be the bastard who stole my innocence.

All together I was at this convent for two years. I was taught impeccable manners right down to learning how to eat an apple with a knife and fork. However, my ability to lie was never impeded. It was instead sharpened.

Chapter Ten
Securing Our Visas

My mother and I were just biding our time until we could secure our Visas for the United States. At first, we were going to go to Israel, but since the British were still ruling, my mother decided she just couldn't go where fighting and turmoil remained. There were only two places where one could get visas: either in Germany or in Italy. And we certainly weren't going into Germany, so that is how and why we had ended up in Italy.

Inka's passport picture, Rome, 1948.

Frieda's passport picture, Rome, 1948.

The Polish quota for securing visas to the United States was totally exhausted. The Russian quota was still wide open and Momma, once again, was able to acquire phony papers showing us to be of Russian descent.

Once we secured our Visas we confirmed our space on the ship Saturnia. It was May of 1948 when we boarded the ship that would arrive in New York harbor, USA on May 18th.

We were considered 5th class passengers, and housed in the bowels of the ship. The accommodations were dormitory style. The first two days aboard, the ocean was calm because we were on the Mediterranean. After the second day we hit the rough, cold Atlantic Ocean. My mother developed violent sea sickness. There was no administration of medication for our group and Momma was never able to lift her head again until we arrived in America.

Meanwhile, being my precocious nine-year-old self, I had a wonderful time on that ship.

Momma is dead to the world with her nausea. I am totally bored and it is so sad and dreary down here. I am not going to stay down here any longer. I know this ship has much more to offer ... so up I go.

I used my Italian language skills to charm the ship attendants as I climbed my way to first class. A few of the first-class passengers thought I was just adorable and on many occasions I was invited to join them for meals in the first-class dining room. When I walked in, I suddenly realized my clothing was not up to par and I was definitely different.

People are staring at me and I know why ... I don't really belong here. My clothes give me away. But, hey, inside I know

Inka and her mother aboard the Saturnia, heading for the USA.

this is where I want to belong. I will turn on my convent manners, curtsey at the appropriate times and geez ... I hope they don't serve green peppers here!

Unfortunately not all the rotating attendants knew me and I would be harshly redirected back downstairs before I could reach my newly acquired first-class admirers. It became necessary for me to discover alternate routes in order to accomplish my goal – acceptance by the upper-crust.

I had a wonderful trip; freedom and fun, my two favorite "fs". I started feeling like I was no longer connected to a fifth class. I began thinking of myself as a much better fit in first class and could no longer relate to being anything less.

I am free ... I am going to America!

Epilogue

The house suddenly shakes and the windows rattle. A rescue helicopter grazes overhead on its landing pattern. The mere sound ties my stomach into knots and my throat tightens. Standing before my bedroom mirror, I am immediately drawn back in time to my attic mirror. I have never fully left.

As my hand runs across the deep wrinkles and crevices of my face, the reality of my survival brings back the sheer importance of that attic. My still very blue, but tired old eyes, reassure my reflection that those horrors have passed and I can freely step out into the sunshine, unafraid.

Or can I?

Made in the USA
Middletown, DE
26 April 2016